REDEEMED

PRESENTED TO

_____

BY

_____

ON THIS DATE

_____

Sanctify the Lord God in your hearts, and always be
ready to give a defense to everyone who asks you a reason for
the hope that is in you, with meekness and fear.

—1 PETER 3:15

REDEEMED

DEVOTIONS *for the* LONGING SOUL

WILL GRAHAM

THOMAS NELSON
Since 1798

Published in Nashville, Tennessee, by Thomas Nelson. Thomas Nelson is a registered trademark of HarperCollins Christian Publishing, Inc.

Billy Graham quotes taken from previously published material in *Billy Graham in Quotes* and used by permission of the Billy Graham Evangelistic Association.

Photos used by permission of the Billy Graham Evangelistic Association.

Thomas Nelson titles may be purchased in bulk for educational, business, fund-raising, or sales promotional use. For information, please e-mail SpecialMarkets@ThomasNelson.com.

Scripture quotations are taken from the New King James Version®. © 1982 by Thomas Nelson. Used by permission. All rights reserved.

ISBN 978-4002-1013-8 (eBook)

Library of Congress Cataloging-in-Publication Data
ISBN 978-1-4002-1010-7 (HC)

Printed in China
18 19 20 21 22 DSC 10 9 8 7 6 5 4 3 2 1

To my grandfather, Billy Graham, who "changed addresses" shortly after I finished writing this book. He's now home with his Savior, the One whom he proclaimed around the world. I love you, Daddy Bill!

CONTENTS

INTRODUCTION

FOR HE SATISFIES THE LONGING
SOUL, AND FILLS THE HUNGRY
SOUL WITH GOODNESS.

— PSALM 107:9

*H*ave you ever studied the Bible and had a verse jump out at you? Perhaps you've read it many times before, but one day it catches your eye and impacts you deeply as you meditate on it.

As I was preparing to write this devotional book, I happened upon such a verse. Psalm 107:9 says, "For He satisfies the longing soul, and fills the hungry soul with goodness." It seems so simple, and yet it is incredibly profound.

As I've traveled the globe to share the good news of Jesus Christ, I've seen "longing souls" from every walk of life. In the most affluent cities where they truly believe they have it all, to the back alleys of third world nations, people are desperate for hope and goodness.

Deep inside their souls they are hungering for something, but they don't know what that is. They're vainly trying to satisfy that empty space that asks: Is there more to life than this? What is my purpose? What is the meaning of life? Is there hope or order in the chaos? Does God love me or even care about me?

Some pursue good deeds, positive social work, mentoring, or donating money to worthy causes. Others try to overcome the void by throwing themselves into their relationships, jobs, or hobbies. Unfortunately there are many who seek futile fulfillment in destructive vices that only bring more sadness and suffering.

But the Bible tells us that God—only God—can fill the void inside of us. Not only that, He satisfies that longing with goodness—not more pain or hopelessness and not more chores, requirements, or broken promises; no, He satisfies us with His goodness!

As we begin this journey together, I pray that you will be inspired in some cases and challenged in others. I pray that your faith will grow and that your eyes will be opened to the eternal needs of those around you.

Most of all I pray that you will draw closer to the God who satisfies your longing soul and fills your hungry soul with His goodness.

COMMUNION

FOR THROUGH HIM WE BOTH
HAVE ACCESS BY ONE SPIRIT
TO THE FATHER.

—EPHESIANS 2:18

I can remember the exact moment when I realized that there was something different about my grandfather. I was in elementary school, and one of the teachers put her hands on my shoulders and told another teacher, "This is Billy Graham's grandson." I wondered how on earth she knew my grandfather.

You see, we—my brothers, sister, and I—were raised in the mountains of North Carolina, a world away from the large audiences that would gather to hear my grandfather's messages. We were good kids. We would get into mischief but were mostly harmless.

One Sunday morning when I was nearly six years old, I sat next to my parents in the pew at church. I noticed that they were passing out a snack and everybody was getting a bite. I couldn't be sure, but it looked like it might be a bit of bread and a cup of grape juice.

I was excited! I was hungry and wanted a snack!

As the tray of bread came by, I reached out to take a piece. Suddenly my dad reached up and smacked the back of my hand, not hard enough to hurt but enough that I understood the message and let the plate pass. I couldn't figure it out. I had been good all service (which isn't necessarily easy for a young boy who is used to running around the mountainside). I could only assume that my parents were afraid I would spill it on the church carpet.

> *"Your salvation depends on what [Christ] has done for you, not on what you do for Him. It isn't your hold on God that saves you; it's His hold on you."*
>
> —BILLY GRAHAM

That afternoon my dad took me up to my room and began to explain to me what communion is. He shared that it's a time of remembrance for those who have accepted Jesus as Savior. He told me about what Jesus did for me on the cross. He explained how Jesus died for my sins and that I can spend eternity with Him in heaven.

That was the day my dad used communion to explain the gospel, and I surrendered my life to Jesus.

I didn't have all the answers. I didn't understand the whole Bible. But I did know a few things. I knew that I had sinned; I knew that Jesus took my sins to the cross; I knew that He conquered the grave; and I knew that I wanted a relationship with Him as my Savior.

You see, the fact that I was a good kid and that my last name was Graham didn't mean anything in the scope of eternity. Being Billy Graham's grandson and sitting still in church on Sunday morning was not enough to gain entrance into heaven.

Similarly, you may be the pastor's son or daughter. You may be a deacon or Sunday school superintendent, but your family lineage and good works cannot save you either.

Rather, the decision I made that day with childlike faith was what secured my eternity with Christ.

It's that moment of surrender that has allowed me a lifetime of joy, peace, and purpose in this world and the hope of salvation when my days here are done. Jesus can and will save you as you seek His forgiveness and begin a relationship with Him.

Can you remember a time when you surrendered your life to Jesus? If the answer is no, what is holding you back from doing so?

Dear Jesus, I know that I'm a sinner. I'm sorry for my sins. I believe that You died to pay the punishment for my sins. Please be the Lord of my life. In Your name. Amen.

photo caption: Will with his grandfather, Billy Graham, at a Crusade in Baltimore, Maryland, 1981

Daddy Bill

He brought them out
and said, "Sirs, what must I
do to be saved?"

—ACTS 16:30

When you're a ten-year-old boy, getting to see your grandfather is one of the greatest things in the world.

On this particular day, I worked my way through the crowded room, my dad right behind me. I had that singular focus and tunnel vision that comes with being a child. I finally saw him—my grandfather surrounded by a mass of people.

I was so excited that I couldn't help myself. I took off running to reach him, wanting nothing more than to give him a hug. Suddenly an arm swung downward and stopped me in my tracks. A big security guard looked at me and said, "Excuse me, but the line is over there."

It wasn't until that moment that I realized that everybody in the room was there to see my grandfather, and I was—in the wording of an elementary-age boy—cutting in line.

I was unsure of what to say or do. Though my dad had been with me before I took off running, I now felt very much alone.

My grandfather turned toward the commotion, and I'll never forget what happened next.

> "Love your children—and let them know you love them. Children who experience love find it far easier to believe God loves them."
> —BILLY GRAHAM

A broad, gracious smile spread across his face. He spread his arms wide open and called me to him, and I lunged into his embrace.

While most know the Billy Graham who preached to massive crowds, met with presidents, or was interviewed on national television, that day many people saw the "private" man that I always called "Daddy Bill." His big, encompassing hug made it feel as if I were the only person in the room.

When I consider the love of God for us, His children, I occasionally think back to that day.

Some philosophies believe in a creator who divinely made the world in which we live and then stepped away so we could fend for ourselves.

I don't believe that. I believe that the Creator of the universe knows my name. He knows my tears and pain. He knows my triumphs and my struggles. He knows the number of hairs on my head.

And guess what? Through it all, He loves me with an eternal, unconditional love. He loves me so much that He gave His Son to die for me.

A broken world that seems to thrive on pain and decay tries to tell me that I shouldn't run to Him, but I know where my Father is and where I need to be. He's standing with His arms open wide, ready to embrace me as I lunge into His awaiting arms.

Today He's ready to embrace you as well!

Dear God, thank You for loving me with an unconditional love and for the blessing of being called Your child. Through every step today— whether there be struggles or successes—hold me close to You. In Jesus' name. Amen.

**Are you running toward God or away from Him?
Are you resting in His embrace?**

photo caption: Franklin Graham, Billy Graham, and two-year-old Will Graham, 1977

PEARL GOODE

*I*n the pages of world history, you won't find many mentions of a lady named Pearl Goode. She never ran for political office, commanded troops, or served as the CEO of a Fortune 500 company.

Rather, Pearl was a widowed nurse in her mid-sixties, living in Pasadena, California, in 1949 when my grandfather came to Los Angeles to hold a crusade.

The very first night, she watched the fiery preacher—at that point a largely unknown young evangelist—share the gospel. As Pearl later recounted in an interview, "That night God laid those boys on my heart as a burden."

After that early crusade, Pearl became a prayer warrior for my grandfather. She would buy a Greyhound bus ticket to wherever he was holding an event, quietly check into a nearby motel, and immediately begin praying. Pearl estimated that she covered forty-eight thousand miles by bus, simply to pray for the crusades.

Even later in life when Pearl could no longer travel, or when my grandfather was preaching overseas, she would make it a point to know exactly when he would be preaching, and she would spend those exact moments in prayer.

In an address he gave in 1994, my grandfather said, "She prayed all night many nights, and I could sense the presence and power of that prayer. When she died, I felt it."

We must never underestimate the power of prayers lifted up by wonderful saints like Pearl. Prayer is vital in developing our relationship with our Savior and in building up and supporting others through the work of the Holy Spirit.

> *"True prayer is a way of life, not just for use in cases of emergency. Make it a habit, and when the need arises you will be in practice."*
> — BILLY GRAHAM

The Bible places great importance on prayer: Bless those who curse you, pray for those who mistreat you (Luke 6:28). Be joyful in hope, patient in affliction, faithful in prayer (Romans 12:12). Do not be anxious about anything, but in every situation, by prayer and petition, with thanksgiving, present your requests to God (Philippians 4:6).

These aren't merely pleasant suggestions. I view these as commands to follow in our daily Christian walk. Our Lord knows that only by daily conversation with Him can we live in peace and freedom. Just like Pearl and her prayers for my grandfather's crusades, our prayers can allow others to experience the power of God.

With all of the distractions of life, we often struggle to make prayer a daily priority. Could today be the day when we recognize the need and give our time to God? I guarantee that if you do, you'll see the fruit of this special time almost immediately as He begins to work in and through you!

Dear Lord, thank You for the blessing of being able to come to You in prayer, and forgive me for those times when my focus was elsewhere and I neglected to spend time with You. Make me a prayer warrior who prays without ceasing. I love You, Lord. In Jesus' name I pray. Amen.

Have you experienced the power of prayer, either yours or others? When?

photo caption: Pearl Goode

ELEMENTARY ASSIGNMENT

"YOU DID NOT CHOOSE ME, BUT I CHOSE YOU AND APPOINTED YOU THAT YOU SHOULD GO AND BEAR FRUIT, AND THAT YOUR FRUIT SHOULD REMAIN, THAT WHATEVER YOU ASK THE FATHER IN MY NAME HE MAY GIVE YOU."

—JOHN 15:16

This is going to be a fun, I thought, as the teacher instructed my third-grade class to draw a picture of what we wanted to be when we grew up.

We all tangled over the markers and crayons, and then hunched around the desks diligently plotting the course of our young lives.

I glanced around the room and could quickly see that most of the other boys wanted to be National Football League quarterbacks. Pictures of Joe Montana and Dan Marino, two of the great players of the day, were being drawn with earnestness. Elsewhere there were hand-scribbled pigskins and the big blue star of the Dallas Cowboys.

Looking back on it, our class must have really loved football!

I'm a huge fan of the sport as well, but when it came to my life, I knew I'd never play in the NFL. Rather, as I started drawing, I found myself tracing out a David Clark aviation headset and an open Bible.

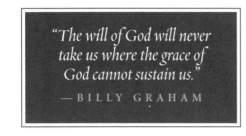

"The will of God will never take us where the grace of God cannot sustain us."

— BILLY GRAHAM

Simply put, I wanted to do what my dad did. I wanted to fly around the world and tell people about Jesus.

Why do I share this story? I'm certainly not trying to pretend I was some sort of a super-spiritual wonder kid. My brothers and I caused enough mischief in our day to put that idea to rest!

Rather, it's to say that from a very early point in my life I was already sensing God's calling and direction, pointing me toward a life in ministry.

I had no idea what that meant at the time. In third grade, I couldn't have begun to tell you if I would be a missionary, a bi-vocational pastor, a Christian relief worker, an evangelist, or in some other form of ministry. I just knew that I was being called.

And, my friends, just as God called me into ministry, if you are a believer and a follower of Christ, He has called you as well. Perhaps your mission field is the public school where you teach, the hospital where you serve, or the office where you work. Maybe your ministry is to your clients or your employees.

Romans 12 tells us that we are collectively different parts of the same body, and we've each been equipped for different work. We may be teachers, encouragers, givers, or leaders. The key component, however, is that God is the One who gives us the calling, and He has prepared us uniquely for it.

If you are reading this and can't think of your calling, seek God for guidance. Prayerfully ask Him to reveal it to you. I truly believe that He will quickly show you the special gifts He has already given you, and how they can be used in service to Him.

If you've learned your calling already, I challenge you to chase after it as a service unto God. Be where you are supposed to be, do what you're supposed to do, and allow God to work through you for the sake of the kingdom.

Do you remember when you were called by God?
Where has He led you to serve?

When I Grow Up

I want to be a missionary because I love Jesus, and I want to be an airplane pilot so I can go to different countries and spread Jesus's word. Well, my dad is a missionary. He spreads Jesus's word, and he is an airplane pilot. My dad works at Samarita Purse.

William Franklin Graham

4+h

Dear God, I know You have a plan and a calling for my life. Please show me, and guide every step as I seek to serve You. Equip me as only You can. In Jesus' name. Amen.

photo caption: The written portion of Will's elementary assignment, which accompanied the picture he drew

CAN I TELL YOU ABOUT JESUS?

BUT SANCTIFY THE LORD GOD IN YOUR HEARTS,
AND ALWAYS BE READY TO GIVE A DEFENSE TO
EVERYONE WHO ASKS YOU A REASON FOR THE
HOPE THAT IS IN YOU, WITH MEEKNESS AND FEAR.

—1 PETER 3:15

*D*enise stepped off the bus in the dark of night in the small outback mining town of Broken Hill, Australia. After catching a few hours of sleep in the bus station, she planned to begin a treacherous journey, hitchhiking 320 miles across the unforgiving landscape to Adelaide.

We had just wrapped up an evangelistic outreach in town, and that morning we were having a celebration of sorts in a local coffee house, thanking God for the way that He had moved in the community. Unbeknownst to me, Denise walked through the door, drawn by the commotion.

Denise began a conversation with Margaret, the wife of the man who served as chairperson of our event in Broken Hill. Filled with the confidence that came from watching many respond to the gospel that weekend, Margaret boldly asked Denise, "Can I tell you about Jesus?"

At the mention of the name Jesus, tears formed in Denise's eyes. Gently, Margaret began sharing about the love of Christ, and soon had the opportunity to pray with Denise as she accepted Jesus as her Savior.

> "A true messenger lives a burdened life. If he is the Lord's vessel, he carries in his heart a burden for souls none can share but those who know it firsthand."
>
> — BILLY GRAHAM

Before it was all done, another blessing awaited Denise. One of the believers in the coffee house, learning of Denise's plan, anonymously purchased a plane ticket to Adelaide, saving her the potentially deadly hike across the outback.

Denise left that day with both physical and eternal security, her path to Adelaide paid for by a generous benefactor, and the wages of her sins paid for by the free gift of Jesus Christ and His sacrifice on the cross.

There are a couple of lessons to be learned from Margaret's interaction with Denise.

First, there is value in being prepared when God opens a door to share the gospel with others. Many people will say that they feel ill-equipped to share their faith, but it doesn't have to be that way. No, you may not have all the answers, but it's eternally important to be Spirit-filled by spending time in the Word and in prayer. God has promised that He'll give you the words to say (Luke 12:12).

Second, it doesn't matter how much time you spend studying

and building relationships with people if you aren't willing to ask the question that Margaret asked: "Can I tell you about Jesus?"

Can you imagine if God had opened the door for Margaret to share the hope of Jesus, but rather than being prepared (as instructed in 1 Peter 3:15) she had wilted? It's almost assured that the two women would never cross paths again, and that opportunity would have been lost. Eternity would have been altered.

Watch for the open doors that God provides, and be ready to walk through them. Don't let your personal Denise walk away without asking, "Can I tell you about Jesus?"

Has God been preparing you to share
His love with someone you know?

Lord Jesus, we give You praise for
people like Margaret who are willing
to boldly step out in faith to share
Your love with those who need it. Help
me to recognize opportunities that
You place in my path, and give me the
words to say. In Jesus' name. Amen.

photo caption: Will with Denise in Broken Hill, Australia,
holding the sign she was going to use to hitchhike to Adelaide

RUTH GRAHAM

FOR I CONSIDER THAT THE SUFFERINGS OF THIS
PRESENT TIME ARE NOT WORTHY TO BE COMPARED
WITH THE GLORY WHICH SHALL BE REVEALED IN US.

—ROMANS 8:18

My grandmother, Ruth Graham, was many things. She was an accomplished poet and author. She was a practical joker who loved to laugh, her bright eyes dancing as she sought mischief. She was fiercely generous and gracious, sheltering the needy and making everyone feel welcomed and loved. In fact, she could make a princess and a panhandler feel at home in the same room.

In my grandparents' house was a room that was my grandmother's sanctuary. It was where she would write, pray, and study. She had multiple translations of the Bible laid out on a desk, each with extra-large margins so she could jot notes as she pored through God's Word.

On the walls above the desk hung family photos and a simple wreath of Jerusalem thorns, much like the one that was forced onto Jesus' head during His crucifixion.

This room was also where my grandmother would bravely face her final days on earth, struggling against the debilitating pain that was a constant and unwelcome companion. She never grumbled about her struggles, though you would occasionally see her wince as the suffering overwhelmed her. Rather, she would look up at the crown of thorns on the wall and say, "If my Savior could endure so much for me, I have nothing to complain about."

> *"The Bible teaches us that we are to be patient in suffering. Tears become telescopes to heaven, bringing eternity a little closer."*
> — BILLY GRAHAM

I have to admit, I wish that pain and suffering weren't a part of life. Life would be so much easier, wouldn't it? Some days it is very hard to accept the harsh realities of the world—the hurt, uncertainty, sin, and suffering.

However, it's important to note two things:

First, Christ—as well as the early disciples and believers throughout history—faced suffering. This suffering was not just the kind associated with old age and the broken vessels that are our human bodies. No, they faced great suffering for taking a stand for the faith. Many have endured deep pain that only ended when their time on earth was done and they were finally able to partake in glory.

Second, regardless of the struggles we face as we call upon the Lord and put our eternal hope in Him, the trials and pain of this world are but a fleeting shadow in the scope of eternity with our Savior.

As Paul wrote in his letter to the Romans, "For I consider that the sufferings of this present time are not worthy to be compared with the glory which shall be revealed in us" (8:18).

No matter what life throws at you today, find joy in the Lord and in His eternal promises!

Dear Lord, today and the days to come will not be perfect. Along with the mountaintop experiences, I know there will also be valleys I must walk through. There will be joys and there will be struggles. Help me to keep my eyes on You. I pray this in Jesus' name. Amen.

In what ways can you find the joy of the Lord today even in the midst of difficult circumstances?

photo caption: Ruth Graham's room

Easter
Opportunities

"Now when they bring you to the syna-
gogues and magistrates and authorities, do
not worry about how or what you should
answer, or what you should say. For the
Holy Spirit will teach you in that very
hour what you ought to say."

—LUKE 12:11-12

*S*everal years ago Kendra and I paid an Easter visit to my grand-parents at their house in Montreat, North Carolina.

On our way back home that afternoon, we pulled into a little gas station on the south side of US Route 70 to fuel up and be on our way. I patiently stood in line while the people in front of me made friendly conversation with the clerk behind the counter.

"Nothing's free anymore!" the man chuckled as he handed over the money to pay for his purchase.

Something incredible happened at that moment. Immediately God told me to speak, and He even provided the words to say.

The Holy Spirit led me to share the gospel with these people, saying, "Tell them what Easter is all about, how God paid the debt for you through His Son, Jesus, and in return He offers you salvation for free."

My friends, that's what I should have said.

Sadly I kept that proclamation to myself. I regret it to this day. God called me to share His hope on that glorious Easter with people who likely needed to hear it, but I disobeyed Him and kept it silently in my heart.

Frankly I chickened out.

The very first Bible verse that I memorized as a young boy remains one of my favorites. Luke 12:12 says, "For the Holy Spirit will teach you in that very hour what you ought to say."

And it's 100 percent true. The Holy Spirit guided me in what to say, but when it was time to step forward and follow His leading, I didn't do it. I disobeyed.

I made a covenant with God that day that if I ever felt Him speaking through me again, I would share it boldly and not hold back. Who knows? Sharing the words God gives us may be the difference between someone spending an eternity in heaven or in hell—the difference between a life of hope and a life of discouragement and despair.

I encourage you to listen to God as He speaks to you and to be His mouthpiece as He speaks through you. We need to take every opportunity available to us to share His saving message.

God is ready to use each of us for His kingdom if we'll only make ourselves available. Are you ready?

"I am convinced that when a man sincerely searches for God with all his heart, God will reveal Himself in some way."

—Billy Graham

Dear God, forgive me for being hard-hearted or for purposely turning away when I hear You calling. Use me for Your glory. Provide open hearts and open doors to share Your love and the hope that I have in You. I pray this in Jesus' name. Amen.

Forest Home

"But seek first the kingdom of God
and His righteousness, and all these
things shall be added to you."

—MATTHEW 6:33

*I*f you've followed my grandfather's preaching through the years, you probably have a picture of him in your head.

Maybe it's the traveling evangelist they called "God's Machine Gun" as he rattled out verse after verse with blistering passion, prowling the stage while swinging his hands in the air. Perhaps your recollection is of "God's Ambassador" of the 1970s and 1980s, graying hair and confident calls for people to respond to Christ while there's still time. If you're of a younger generation, you may picture the elder statesman, the great-grandfather who would cling to the podium as he spoke softly with the authority of the Holy Word.

You probably don't picture a young man who, in the autumn of 1949, was going through a great test of his faith, unsure of himself and his calling. But that's exactly the struggle that gripped Billy Graham, soon to turn thirty-one, as he made his way to Forest Home retreat center in California.

A particularly difficult evangelistic rally in Pennsylvania, soul-searching regarding his role and future as the president of Northwestern Schools in Minnesota, and a contemporary who encouraged him to doubt the truth of the Bible all collided into a supreme crisis of conscience.

> "I pondered the attitude of Christ toward the Scriptures. He loved those sacred writings and quoted from them constantly. Never once did He intimate that they could be wrong."
> —BILLY GRAHAM

Frankly he was having a hard time answering the difficult questions posed by his friend, and starting to question the Word of God as well.

Though nobody could have known it at the time, the visit to Forest Home would define my grandfather one way or the other. It was the fulcrum, and the only question was which way the balance would tip.

You see, though he was there to speak, my grandfather spent a great deal of time at Forest Home studying the Bible and in prayer, pleading to God for direction. As he pored through the Scripture, he kept seeing the same phrase repeated throughout: "Thus sayeth the Lord." While my grandfather had always accepted the authority of the Bible, those four words finally sparked the realization in his heart that the book he held in his hand was not the work of man, but the divinely inspired, eternal, and powerful voice of God.

As my grandfather later shared, one night at Forest Home he walked out into the woods and set his Bible on a stump, where he cried out, confessing his questions and doubts before falling to his knees as the Holy Spirit moved in him.

As he rose from the ground, he felt the power and presence of God.

As Christians we often want to pretend that everything in our lives is great. We force the smile onto our face, pushing down the pain to hide our internal struggles. The fact of the matter, however, is that even Billy Graham battled against doubts.

The question is, how are we going to handle these crises of faith that arrive in our lives?

My grandfather could have become frustrated and walked away. He even thought about leaving preaching and his work at Northwestern to become a dairy farmer like his dad.

Matthew 6:33 says, "But seek first the kingdom of God and His righteousness, and all these things shall be added to you." This is what my grandfather did. Rather than giving up, my grandfather fully and completely sought God—His will, His guidance, and His Word. Because he did, millions of people were impacted for eternity.

My friends, be encouraged, and seek your answers in the Word of God. He was there for my grandfather in his valley of doubts, and He's there for you today.

What are you struggling with today? Will you draw near to God, finding your answers and peace in Him?

Dear Lord, in my life I may have doubts, but I also know that You are the author of my life, guiding me day by day. Help me to seek You above all else. In Jesus' name. Amen.

photo caption: Billy Graham speaking at Forest Home

ESTABLISH A
HERITAGE OF LOVE

AND THESE WORDS WHICH I COMMAND YOU
TODAY SHALL BE IN YOUR HEART. YOU SHALL
TEACH THEM DILIGENTLY TO YOUR CHILDREN,
AND SHALL TALK OF THEM WHEN YOU SIT IN YOUR
HOUSE, WHEN YOU WALK BY THE WAY, WHEN YOU
LIE DOWN, AND WHEN YOU RISE UP.

—DEUTERONOMY 6:6-7

*N*ight after night an Australian bus driver stopped to collect a joyful throng of worship-filled riders. He didn't try to hide his disgust and contempt. An alcoholic, his marriage and life were falling apart. He saw no reason for the happiness that his riders expressed.

The year was 1959 and the driver—a man named Ron—was one of many who were hired to shuttle attendees back and forth from my grandfather's crusade in Sydney. This proved to be a major undertaking, with nearly one million people taking part in the weeks-long outreach.

Ron would drop the riders off at the Sydney Showground and sit with a scowl on his face until he had to open the doors and let them back onto the bus after the program. His irritation would only grow as his passengers sang hymns and praises for what God was doing in their city.

Unexpectedly, a miracle took place.

Ron's wife was invited to the crusade by a friend, and she surrendered her life to Christ! The following week at his wife's urging, Ron sat in the same venue to which he had angrily transported many others.

> *"We need to place God at the center of our family. . . . As a family, we need to walk with God daily."*
> —BILLY GRAHAM

This broken shell of a man heard the gospel and decided that it wasn't for him. Then he heard my grandfather call out, "God's speaking to a man here tonight!"

At that moment Ron heard another voice—one inside him urging, "Go!" So he went.

God radically transformed Ron's life. He healed him of his addictions. He mended his broken marriage. He even called Ron into ministry. And the couple raised their children in a loving Christian home.

While their salvation and the restoration that Ron and his wife received are eternally important, it's that last part of the equation that I often think of when I consider this story: his children and lineage.

Rather than growing up in a broken home, his children were nurtured in the faith, and ultimately they each went into ministry as well. They married and had families of their own, and those children—Ron's grandchildren—chose to follow Christ.

What potentially could have been generations of hurt and scars became generations of light, hope, and faith. It was all because in 1959, a young husband and wife said yes to Jesus.

You see, we are all leaving a legacy. How will your children and grandchildren remember you? Some may leave a heritage of love and peace, while others pass along bitterness and anger. Our heirloom could be a memory of joy in the Lord or of a lifetime spent chasing the things of this world.

Now please hear me when I say that you can't make your children's decisions for them. They will choose their own path. But I would encourage you to always model a life devoted to Christ, seeking righteousness, pursuing prayer, and exhibiting grace.

Others are watching and will take notice, and generations may be impacted because of your faith.

What legacy are you leaving for your
children and grandchildren?

*Dear God, help me to leave
a legacy of hope and joy for
my family. Draw me so close
that others will see You in
me. In Jesus' name. Amen.*

photo caption: 1959 Crusade in Sydney, Australia

PURPOSE FULFILLED

"I KNOW THE THOUGHTS THAT I
THINK TOWARD YOU, SAYS THE LORD,
THOUGHTS OF PEACE AND NOT OF EVIL, TO
GIVE YOU A FUTURE AND A HOPE."

—JEREMIAH 29:11

*Y*ou may have a pen sitting next to you right now. If so, pick it up and look at it for a second.

What is the purpose of that pen? Unless you have a special pen that I'm not familiar with, the odds are good that the purpose of your pen is to write.

Now, set the pen back down on the table. What does it do? Is it accomplishing anything? Is it scribbling on the pages of this book, or in the margins of your Bible? Not likely.

What if you were to set a nice, clean sheet of white paper next to it? Now you have a pen and paper. That's all you need. Is the pen writing now? Is it fulfilling its purpose?

No. In order for the pen to fulfill its purpose, it requires your involvement and direction. That pen needs you to pick it up, press it against the paper, and begin to move it. It can be said that the pen only fulfills its purpose when it's in its master's hand.

I like to use this illustration when I'm sharing the gospel because we are very much like that pen sitting in front of you. We were made for a purpose, but we can only fulfill that purpose when we're in the Master's hand.

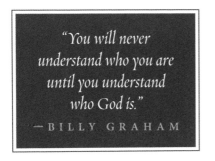

"You will never understand who you are until you understand who God is."
—BILLY GRAHAM

In fact, many people spend their entire lives searching for their purpose. They'll try to find it in their work, their relationships, or their vices. They'll chase empty dreams and broken promises, and ultimately come away unfulfilled because they're missing the key element. They're a pen laying on the table, not in the Master's hand.

So, what is your purpose? Have you ever thought about it? Perhaps you feel that it's to be the best mother or father possible for your children. Maybe your purpose is to lead a ministry or bring joy to others.

These are all fantastic things and I'm glad you're doing them, but I believe that those missions grow *out of* your purpose. Rather, your one purpose in life is to have a relationship with Jesus and to worship Him with all you are. You see, it's only when that happens—when you're in your Master's hand—that your purpose is fulfilled.

As you fully understand and embrace your purpose as a child of the King, you will begin to find joy and peace. Your focus will be on the things of God and less on the worries of man. Frustrations, jealousy, and dissension will give way to everlasting fulfillment.

Dear God, help me to find
my purpose in You. I place
my life in the Master's hand.
In Jesus' name. Amen.

As you embrace your purpose, what is God
leading you to do for His kingdom?

photo caption: 1959 Crusade in Sydney, Australia

LOUIS ZAMPERINI

LET ALL BITTERNESS, WRATH, ANGER, CLAMOR,
AND EVIL SPEAKING BE PUT AWAY FROM YOU, WITH
ALL MALICE. AND BE KIND TO ONE ANOTHER,
TENDERHEARTED, FORGIVING ONE ANOTHER,
EVEN AS GOD IN CHRIST FORGAVE YOU.

—EPHESIANS 4:31-32

*L*ouis Zamperini was an Olympic runner destined for greatness as he prepared for the 1940 Summer Games in Tokyo, only to have them cancelled as World War II enveloped the globe.

Rather than winning gold, Louis joined the military to serve his country aboard a B-24, taking part in several successful bombing missions in the Pacific Theater.

One fateful day, while on a search and rescue mission in an old dilapidated airplane, Louis's crew crashed in the ocean. Everybody on board was killed except Louis, his pilot Allen "Phil" Phillips, and tail gunner Francis "Mac" McNamara. The men floated in a life raft for forty-seven days (a record for the longest time adrift without rescue), living off the rare bird or fish they could catch with their bare hands—and all while dodging sharks and the occasional strafing run by Japanese warplanes. Mac didn't survive, dying along the way.

Eventually Louis and Phil reached shore, but it was by way of an enemy Japanese ship that pulled them from the sea. From there, a bad dream became an utter nightmare. Months of starvation, disease, psychological trauma, unimaginable living conditions, and daily abuse at the hands of sadistically brutal prison guards reduced Louis to a shell of the once-great athlete. The list of regular and ongoing assaults that Louis endured would shock and nauseate you.

One of the few things that kept Louis alive during his horrifying ordeal was the dream of murdering his captors. In fact, one of the men was so cruel that Louis and the other prisoners hatched a plan to kill him, even if the punishment would be their own executions.

> *"In one bold stroke, forgiveness obliterates the past and permits us to enter the land of new beginnings."*
> —BILLY GRAHAM

Amazingly, Louis survived and made it home to California, only to find himself living in a new prison—one of post-traumatic stress disorder, nightmares, and alcoholism. He was a broken man in a downward spiral.

Why do I share this story? Because something amazing happened. At his wife's urging, he attended my grandfather's historic 1949 Los Angeles Crusade, and there he placed his faith in Christ. Miraculously, his nightmares and need for alcohol were gone. He fully and completely forgave his captors, the very people he had dreamt of killing. He even traveled back to Japan to meet with some of them face-to-face so he could share the hope and love of Jesus with them.

The story of Louis Zamperini is one of the greatest examples of forgiveness that I've found outside of the Bible.

Nobody could have expected to survive the torture that Louis endured, let alone recover from it. And most people would understand completely if Louis had held a grudge against his tormenters until the day he died. After all, he was treated subhumanly, beaten, and starved within an inch of his life.

It took time and the intervention of Jesus Christ and the gospel in Louis's life before he was able to fully move forward beyond the suffering he had endured.

I can't speak for you, but I can tell you that even as a believer and an evangelist, I still struggle with forgiveness even though the injustices that affect me are a far cry from the terror endured by Louis Zamperini.

However, let's draw inspiration from Louis's story and seek the freedom that comes with forgiving those who have hurt us. Louis's life is proof that it can be done, and it's worth doing.

Are you holding on to anger or pain? What's stopping you from offering forgiveness?

Lord Jesus, You know the pains and struggles in my life. You know the hurt in my heart left there by others. Help me to forgive them as You have forgiven me. In Jesus' name. Amen.

photo caption: Billy Graham with Louis Zamperini

FREEBIRD

BUT WHEN HE SAW THE MULTITUDES, HE
WAS MOVED WITH COMPASSION FOR THEM,
BECAUSE THEY WERE WEARY AND SCATTERED,
LIKE SHEEP HAVING NO SHEPHERD. THEN HE
SAID TO HIS DISCIPLES, "THE HARVEST TRULY IS
PLENTIFUL, BUT THE LABORERS ARE FEW."

— MATTHEW 9:36-37

*M*y friend Todd and I were in a small Texas town to hold an evangelistic crusade, when Todd pulled up to the stoplight and saw a man by the side of the road asking for spare change. His weathered skin and long, sun-bleached hair were testaments to a hard life spent enduring the elements. As God moved in Todd's heart, he steered his car off to the shoulder of the road and waved the man over. They chatted for a while, and Todd invited him to the outreach.

Though the panhandler had plenty to say about "those Christians," he still agreed to go.

I had no idea that any of this was taking place while I was backstage preparing to preach that evening. That particular program was geared toward young people, so when I offered the invitation to make a commitment to Jesus, I quickly noticed the older gentleman walking forward. He stood head and shoulders above everybody else—a stark contrast to the sea of teenagers around him.

The man gave his life to Jesus Christ that night, finding hope not just in this world but for eternity.

Freebird was his name, taken from the Lynyrd Skynyrd song. As his tired face beamed with love and joy, he told Todd, "They call me Freebird, but I've never felt free in my life until tonight."

When the Holy Spirit nudged Todd to stop alongside the road, he could have buried the thought and driven away. And when Freebird started bad-mouthing Christians, Todd could have moved on. But he didn't do either of those things. Because of that, Freebird's eternity was forever changed.

> *"The Spirit goes ahead of us when we witness—preparing the way, giving us the words, and granting us courage."*
> —BILLY GRAHAM

How often do we watch our coworkers, family, friends, and neighbors—even the man asking for extra change on the street corner—struggle through life without sharing with them that they can have true hope for eternity? We're always too busy or too timid or too jaded to share the love and peace we've found. Let's not miss those opportunities.

My friends, people need the Lord! I pray we will have an urgency in our spirits to share Him with others and that He would allow us to see the miracle of people finding true freedom in Christ. We must remember that eternity is at stake.

I pray that I never forget what Todd and Freebird taught me, and I pray that you, too, will be challenged to reach out to people who need the Lord.

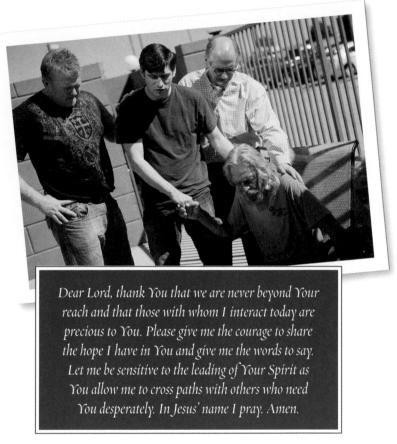

Dear Lord, thank You that we are never beyond Your reach and that those with whom I interact today are precious to You. Please give me the courage to share the hope I have in You and give me the words to say. Let me be sensitive to the leading of Your Spirit as You allow me to cross paths with others who need You desperately. In Jesus' name I pray. Amen.

When you come across people today who need to know Jesus, will you step out of your comfort zone and engage with them in a meaningful way?

photo caption: Will and his team pray with Freebird in Terrell, Texas

HEAVEN IS HOME

As it is written: "Eye has not seen, nor ear heard, nor have entered into the heart of man the things which God has prepared for those who love Him."

—1 CORINTHIANS 2:9

My grandfather was one of the most heaven-focused people I've ever met.

Though Bible verses such as 1 Corinthians 2:9 make it clear that we have no understanding of the magnitude of "the things which God has prepared for those who love Him," for my grandfather, heaven was not a distant and inaccessible realm.

Especially in his final years on earth, heaven was just as real as the house in which he lived. It would be his new home where he would reside once his journey here was complete.

Long before he slipped quietly into eternity on February 21, 2018, my grandfather made the following proclamation about his own passing:

"One day you're going to hear that Billy Graham has died," he said, somber and serious, but also brimming with hope and peace. "But don't believe it! For on that day I will be more alive than ever before. I will have just changed addresses!"

You see, my grandfather spent decades proclaiming the reality of heaven and the narrow road that leads there. Just as an ambassador promotes his home country and pursues its best interests in a foreign land, my grandfather traveled the world as a representative of Christ, sharing and promoting the hope and glory in the heavenly realm for those who call upon the name of Jesus.

I believe heaven became increasingly real to him as he aged well into his nineties. The things of this world—especially his beloved wife (my grandmother, Ruth, who made her own final journey to heaven in 2007) and most of his friends—had already gone on ahead of him. He once joked that he had lived so long that his friends in heaven would be wondering where he was!

In many ways this world was no longer home and heaven was clearly where his heart resided, even before the glorious morning when he passed from this broken realm into God's presence.

"My home is in heaven. I'm just passing through this world."
— BILLY GRAHAM

I assume that most of you who are reading this are younger than my grandfather, but you may be dealing with a terminal disease. You may have lost a loved one recently. You may be clinging to the hope of heaven as your anchor in the storm.

If this is you, bless you. I pray that you're finding the peace of God as you walk this valley.

In addition to focusing on the *hope* of heaven, I would encourage you to cling to the *reality* of heaven as well. Like my grandfather, understand that heaven is a very real place where you will reside for eternity with your Savior.

But it's not just a different address. This very real place will be something so far beyond what our human minds can begin to comprehend. There will be no mourning or pain, hunger or thirst. There will be a place specially prepared for you. The old will be gone, and all things will be made new!

If you've surrendered your life to Jesus as your Savior, don't fear death. Instead, anxiously anticipate heaven and the promise of eternity with Him.

Do you view heaven as a hope or as a reality?

*Dear God, though my mind can't begin
to comprehend Your realm, help me
to live each day with an understanding
of the reality of heaven. Keep my eyes
fixed on You as I journey through the
darkness of this life and toward the
light of eternity. In Jesus' name. Amen.*

photo caption: Billy Graham at his home in the North Carolina mountains

From Thunder Bay to God's Plan

"For My thoughts are not your thoughts, nor are your ways My ways," says the Lord. "For as the heavens are higher than the earth, so are My ways higher than your ways, and My thoughts than your thoughts."

—ISAIAH 55:8-9

*S*everal years ago, my team embarked on a tour across Canada, stopping in small towns to share the gospel in youth-focused meetings. One of the events took place in Thunder Bay, Ontario, a blue-collar city on the Lake Superior shoreline not too far north of the Minnesota-Canada border.

I have to admit that on that particular night, I was discouraged and frustrated. The gathered crowd of teenagers was small, even by our modest expectations.

At the same time, the travel had taken a toll on my body, and I was falling ill. While the band performed, I crossed the street to the local mall to pick up some medicine for my sore throat.

As I looked around, I became even more disappointed. It seemed that there were more kids standing within ten feet of me at the mall than there were in the entire venue next door.

As terrible as it sounds, I passively made the decision to write off the Thunder Bay event. *You're going to have a bad night occasionally,* I reasoned. I'd get through the program and then move on.

But a funny thing happened. Even though I gave up on Thunder Bay, God didn't. After the gospel was shared, 20 percent of the audience—one out of every five kids in attendance—gave their lives to Christ! The crowd wasn't huge, but the response certainly was.

Afterward I wept. I was convicted. By doubting that God would move in Thunder Bay, I also doubted His power to transform the lives and eternities of those kids. God taught me that night that it's not my place to worry about the crowd. My job is to be obedient and preach the good news, letting God work His perfect plan in the lives of those hearing the Word.

Have you ever had a situation in which you just didn't understand God's plan? Perhaps you were hoping and praying for the health or salvation of a loved one, or maybe you were desperate for a new job or the reconciliation of a relationship.

Like me, maybe you were trying to be obedient, but lost sight of the fact that God has His own plan that He is working for His glory.

Isaiah 55:8–9 reminds us that we can't and won't see God's entire plan. We may get to glimpse little pieces of it, as when so many young people responded to the gospel in spite of my doubt and attitude. However, it's important to know that He is in control and is working in a way that is much greater than we can ask or imagine.

"If you have been trying to limit God—stop it! Don't try to confine Him or His works to any single place or sphere. You wouldn't try to limit the ocean."

—Billy Graham

Lord Jesus, thank You for being in control and working Your plan, even when I may not understand it. Though the path may be dark and I cannot see the way, help me to be obedient to Your calling on my life. In Jesus' name. Amen

Have you ever watched God move in the midst of a difficult situation, eventually understanding a small piece of His plan for your life?

SPEAK SOFTLY

A SOFT ANSWER TURNS AWAY WRATH,
BUT A HARSH WORD STIRS UP ANGER.

—PROVERBS 15:1

A few decades ago my grandfather was invited to speak at the inauguration ceremony of a seminary president. While an event of this nature would normally be cause for celebration, this particular meeting promised to be controversial. The incoming president would be leading the seminary back to a more traditional, conservative theology, and this wasn't a particularly popular stance with some faculty.

When my grandfather arrived, he was amazed to find that faculty lined both sides of the walkway leading up to where the induction would be held.

My grandfather was so moved by the display that he graciously shook hands and greeted every person along the way, expressing his gratitude at the show of support. He couldn't have envisioned a greater welcome and outpouring of love than the one that awaited him.

Later, my grandfather exclaimed to the incoming president, "I can't believe they all came out to greet me!"

"Billy," the president responded. "They weren't here to greet you! They were here to protest you!"

I love how God works. My grandfather was a sweet, thoughtful, loving person, who genuinely and deeply cared about others, even if they disagreed with him. In this case, God used my grandfather's naivety to break down walls of anger and hurt, opening the door for reconciliation and healing amid a potentially explosive situation.

Of course, that one moment didn't cure all the problems that existed. No, the seminary still had a number of obstacles to overcome as they journeyed into a new era.

> *"Suppose there was no anger, no profanity, no lying, no grumbling or complaining; suppose there were no dirty stories told, no unjust criticism—what a different world this would be!"*
>
> —BILLY GRAHAM

However, it was proof that it is often more productive to speak softly, love others, and act graciously than it is to get angry and shake a fist. One way leads to constructive compassion, while the other causes people to dig in their heels and prepare for battle.

There are times when you need to stand up for what you believe in. Certain situations and moral stances require an uncompromising boldness as you live for Christ, but the Bible gives you the road map for disagreement in Proverbs 15:1: "A soft answer turns away wrath, but a harsh word stirs up anger."

Do we have disagreements? Yes. Will we always get along with everybody around us? No. But we don't need to be rude or angry. Rather, we should seek to win over others by exhibiting the love and grace of Christ, just as my grandfather did when dealing with the angry faculty. (Even if by accident!)

Lord Jesus, forgive me for the times I've been needlessly confrontational. Help me to love others and see the best in them. Guide me in knowing when it is time to be gracious or when the situation requires that I stand my ground. In all things, I need You. In Jesus' name. Amen.

How will you react to potentially combative issues that arise today?

photo caption: Billy Graham

CHECK YOUR COMPASS

IN ALL YOUR WAYS ACKNOWLEDGE HIM,
AND HE SHALL DIRECT YOUR PATHS.

— PROVERBS 3:6

*I*t was the spring of 1997, and the day had finally come for my first solo cross-country flight. I had been training to be a pilot for some time, and now I would have to show my ability by taking off, landing, and refueling at several different airports on a daylong journey.

I proceeded through all of my checks, accelerated down the runway, and peeled off into the morning sky.

It didn't take me long to realize that I had messed up.

You see, before you take off, it's vitally important to set the gyroscopic compass to your magnetic heading. You must do this every time because without it you have virtually no chance of getting where you're going.

Unfortunately I had been too nervous, and though I thought I had checked each of the many boxes, I failed to set the compass appropriately.

At this point, lifting off into the sky, I had a choice to make. Would I acknowledge my mistake, turn around, set the plane back down on the runway, and do it right? Or would I keep going my own way, trying to figure it out as I went, even if it meant that I would be completely off course?

> "Pride comes from looking only at ourselves; meekness comes through looking at God."
>
> — BILLY GRAHAM

Sadly I let my pride win out. I couldn't bring myself to return to the airfield below me, and I sped ahead into the wide open.

In this case my mistake—followed by my refusal to acknowledge it—did not end in disaster. I was able to level out the plane and use the old floating magnetic compass to dial in my gyroscopic compass while in the air.

But what if I hadn't? What if I had stubbornly refused to accept my mistake and done nothing to correct it? What if I had stacked bad decision on top of bad decision?

Frankly I might not be here to write these pages!

I could have spent hours searching blindly for the right airstrip and eventually run out of fuel. I would not have found the right path—the one that had been laid out for me.

I'm afraid that my sky-high dilemma is an analogy for a common condition that many of us face. You know that you're on the wrong track. You understand that you've made poor decisions. In some cases, it's one bad choice that has disastrous consequences.

And yet you refuse to acknowledge your struggle or your failing. You refuse to land the proverbial plane and reset your trajectory. You blindly stumble along on your own way, even though it's a path that leads to destruction.

Whatever is going on in your life today, please check your spiritual compass and ensure that you're on the right path. It may be a relationship that you know isn't right. Maybe it's an addiction, a sin, or a passion that's become an idol, pulling you away from your Savior. Perhaps you've hurt someone, and it's time to ask for forgiveness.

Regardless, point your compass to Jesus, follow His Word, and set heaven as your destination. Once you have, to paraphrase Proverbs 3:6, "He shall direct your path."

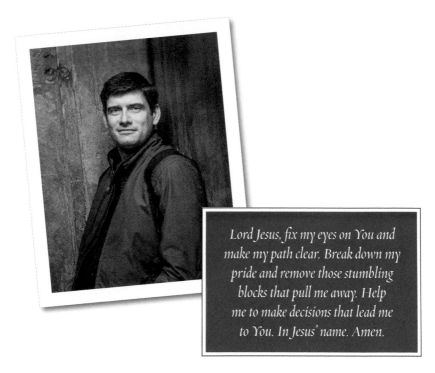

Lord Jesus, fix my eyes on You and make my path clear. Break down my pride and remove those stumbling blocks that pull me away. Help me to make decisions that lead me to You. In Jesus' name. Amen.

Is your compass pointing toward Jesus or have you gotten offtrack?

photo caption: Will Graham

WORTH THE COST

How beautiful upon the mountains are the
feet of him who brings good news, who
proclaims peace, who brings glad tidings of
good things, who proclaims salvation,
who says to Zion, "Your God reigns!"

—ISAIAH 52:7

*M*y grandparents sat down at a table inside the RAI
Amsterdam Convention Centre to visit with an African
man. He was one of thousands of itinerant evangelists taking part in
my grandfather's Amsterdam gathering in 1986, which was meant
to build up and equip the assembled participants in their calling.

My grandfather had a great love for evangelists. While he was
blessed to speak to large arenas of people, he knew that the real
heroes of the faith were the men and women on the front lines who

were taking the gospel door-to-door and town-to-town in hopes that some may be saved.

Based upon his clothing, my grandparents could tell that this man came from humble means. It was clear that he did not have much in this world. Even so, happiness and peace were ever present on the evangelist's face. They learned that the man was from Botswana. He said that there were very few Christians in his country, and his labor was not always fruitful. He persevered, however, because it was his calling from God.

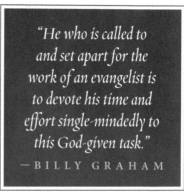

"He who is called to and set apart for the work of an evangelist is to devote his time and effort single-mindedly to this God-given task."
— BILLY GRAHAM

As they continued the discussion, it came out that the man was educated at Cambridge University, one of the most prestigious institutes of higher learning in the world.

He likely could have done anything he chose—led a business, amassed great wealth, or wielded political influence—but instead he was living a very difficult and dangerous life for the sake of the gospel.

Have you ever considered the cost of following Jesus?

For some the cost is social. They make a commitment to Christ and are left behind by friends who have other priorities and forms of recreation.

For others the cost is financial. They must choose which job to take based upon the ethics and integrity of the position and the company.

And then for some there is a real physical cost to be paid. Many people around the world are paying for their faith with their security, their health, and—in some cases—their life. Even in the twenty-first century believers are dying for the sake of their Savior.

In the case of the evangelist who spoke with my grandparents back in 1986, it's safe to assume that his was a combination of all three. He willfully walked away from a financially prosperous life to live the solitary life of an itinerant evangelist in a place that wasn't friendly to the gospel.

But here's the takeaway: he was blessed! He paid the price as an ambassador for the kingdom of God, and he exhibited a peace that many long to find.

There is a cost to following Jesus. You may be paying it right now. But in the scope of eternity—in heaven and on earth—it is worth it!

Consider the price you've paid for following
Christ as your Savior. Is it worth it? Why?

Dear Lord, I commit to follow
You anew today, no matter the
cost. Whatever comes my way,
fill me with Your peace and
hope. In Jesus' name. Amen.

photo caption: RAI Amsterdam Convention Centre

Courage in the Face of Persecution

For to me, to live is Christ,
and to die is gain.

— PHILIPPIANS 1:21

---

*I*t's an honor to be counted worthy to suffer for the name of Christ," the pastor said to me, as we stood on the tsunami-ravaged coastline in southern India.

But he wasn't referring to the massive natural disaster, which struck on December 26, 2004, and claimed the lives of more than 250,000 people.

Instead the pastor was talking about the physical scarring that covered much of his body.

You see, as the pastor was preaching one Sunday, a radical religious group burst into his church and doused him with acid. They burned his body from head to toe, leaving him disfigured.

Miraculously, he survived the attack and has recovered to the point of ministering again to people who desperately need to know the hope of Jesus. However, due to the attack, when he sweats—which is almost constantly given the tropical climate of the area—his body secretes blood.

He showed me the drying blood that coated the fabric inside of his heavy white cotton gown, and he shared that he takes multiple showers a day to cool his body temperature. Sweating blood, the pastor said, is physically excruciating.

> *"While Christians in America have worshipped without the fear or threat of physical abuse for their beliefs, thousands of their brothers in Christ throughout the world have been tortured and martyred for confessing the name of Christ."*
>
> —BILLY GRAHAM

How humbling and convicting! This man of God suffers moment-by-moment, day-by-day, because of his faith. There is no vacation from the pain that surrounds him. When he wakes in the morning and goes to bed at night, the scars, blood, and searing agony are a reminder. At this very moment on the other side of the world, this pastor is in pain.

Given that there's already been one attempt on his life, he must also live with the constant threat of additional bodily harm or death.

And yet he counts it a joy and an honor! Could I say the same thing? No, I'm not sure that I could.

The Bible makes it very clear that we as Christians can expect persecution for our beliefs. In the United States we have been very blessed to have the freedom to worship freely, without the threat of imprisonment or death.

But what if that were no longer the case?

On November 5, 2017, a murderous man with evil in his heart stepped into a church during the Sunday morning service and killed twenty-six people in a small Texas town. Many more were wounded.

While I pray that this type of tragedy stays the exception and not the norm, one must still grapple with the thought of living in a world where your faith could cost you everything.

Is it worth it to you? Is eternity with Jesus more important than the comforts of this world? More important than life itself?

As you seek to learn from this pastor and from martyrs around the world, join me in leaning on the words of the apostle Paul, who was imprisoned for sharing the gospel. In his letter to the church at Philippi, he famously said, "For to me, to live is Christ, and to die is gain" (Philippians 1:21).

Hardship and persecution may come, but if your true hope is in eternity with Christ, you, too, can call it an honor to suffer for Him.

Have you ever faced persecution for your beliefs?
If so, how did you react?

Dear Jesus, there are evil forces in this world that have been harming Your followers since the early church. Protect me and my family. Protect believers around the world. And give me the courage to stand for You in the face of persecution. In Jesus' name. Amen.

photo caption: Will Graham preaching

CHRIST'S SACRIFICE FOR YOU

"GREATER LOVE HAS NO ONE
THAN THIS, THAN TO LAY DOWN
ONE'S LIFE FOR HIS FRIENDS."

—JOHN 15:13

*I*t was the kind of morning that chills your bones. Ice-covered tree limbs crashed down around us as I sat in the woods with Marty, my old seminary classmate who is still one of my closest friends. We'd planned to do some hunting but finally decided to call it a day. The weather was too bad.

As we picked our way through the dense underbrush, bracing against the weather, Marty broke the silence with a very unexpected question.

"Will," he said, "would you give your life for me?"

Mind you, Marty's a big guy, and he was carrying a gun!

I was speechless for a moment. However, as I quickly played the scenario through my head, I knew the answer. "Yes, I believe I would," I responded. And that wasn't just talk. If giving my life would save my friend's life, I truly felt that I could and would do that.

Marty nodded affirmatively. "I'd give up my life for you too," he said. He paused for a second longer before adding, "But I don't think I'd ever be able to trade my child's life for yours."

I suddenly realized where this random question had come from, and it took on much deeper meaning. *Could I give my life for Marty? Of course. Would I ever offer up my daughters or son to die for Marty or for anybody else?* Not a chance! I would protect and defend them with everything in me.

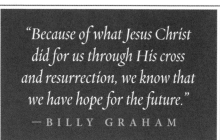

"*Because of what Jesus Christ did for us through His cross and resurrection, we know that we have hope for the future.*"
—BILLY GRAHAM

Marty, of course, was referring to the amazing sacrifice made by God, when He sent His only Son to die for the sins of the world—for your sins and for mine. I'm afraid that as Christians, we hear this so much that we forget or have become numb to the pain behind it.

When you consider this incredible sacrifice from the perspective of parents—who long to protect and love their children above all else—you can begin to understand the pain that was felt not only by Jesus at His crucifixion, but by God the Father as well.

Jesus was God's own Son, a part of Him, whom He sent to die for the sins of mankind.

He walked a lonely road. He was beaten and spat on. He was cursed. He was stabbed in the side, hung on a cross, and mocked. He died a painful and violent death. And He endured all of this for you and me.

God the Father knew the plan and understood the cost of conquering the grave, but it must have pained Him so deeply.

Just by asking me a simple question, Marty had described God's perfect love for each of us, a love so strong that He would make the ultimate sacrifice. Marty couldn't do it. I couldn't either. But God did, and you and I can have eternal hope and life through Him because of it.

Would you give your life for another person?
Does that perspective impact how you think about
Christ's sacrifice for you?

Dear God, never let me forget the price of my salvation. You've given it freely to me, but it cost You dearly. Thank You for Your sacrifice and for the promise of eternity I have in You because of it. In Jesus' name. Amen.

photo caption: Will with his friend Marty

My Grandfather's Best Advice

REJOICE ALWAYS, PRAY WITHOUT CEASING, IN
EVERYTHING GIVE THANKS; FOR THIS IS THE
WILL OF GOD IN CHRIST JESUS FOR YOU.

—1 THESSALONIANS 5:16-18

*P*ray. Pray. Pray," my grandfather said to me, sitting in front of the fireplace in the log home that he and my grandmother built from the ground up in the 1950s. He added, "Study. Study. Study."

He whispered, "Looking back, I wish I had done so much more of both."

I had come to visit him for advice and guidance. I had just been called away from my church to serve with the Billy Graham Evangelistic Association, and I knew this wouldn't be an easy task. I'd be gone from home—from my wife and children—for weeks at a time. I'd be traveling to difficult and spiritually dark places around the world.

After first seeking my heavenly Father through prayer, it made sense to next consult the man who had drawn the blueprint—who had traveled farther and spoken to more people than any other evangelist in human history—my grandfather.

I'll admit that I was expecting a different kind of advice: key verses to use in sermons, hand gestures to drive home a point, or tips on how to invite people to come forward to make a decision for Christ.

Instead, my grandfather's response left me pondering. After all, nearly every time I visited him he was doing one of two things—praying or reading God's Word. He con-

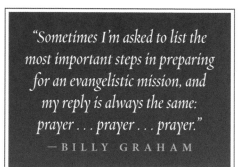

"Sometimes I'm asked to list the most important steps in preparing for an evangelistic mission, and my reply is always the same: prayer . . . prayer . . . prayer."
—BILLY GRAHAM

stantly devoted his time to prayer and study. How could it be that he felt inadequate in these areas?

Perhaps sensing my question, my grandfather explained.

"I wish I knew the Bible as well as your grandmother. She knows it better than anyone I have ever met," he quietly continued. "And we could have done so much more if we had taken fewer speaking engagements and spent more time on our knees in earnest prayer."

And that was it. That was the advice I had sought, and it is guidance that I have carried with me ever since as I've traveled the globe and proclaimed the gospel of Jesus Christ. Not a day goes by when I don't hear my grandfather whisper those words.

Whatever walk of life you are in, I hope that you can hear my grandfather's instruction and take it to heart as well.

You see, you don't have to be an evangelist or a minister to gain incredible, eternal value from time spent in prayer and study. You will be blessed beyond measure as you develop your relationship with God in this way.

Further, it is wise to be careful about doing "too much." We can get so busy that our efforts begin to crowd out our relationship with God. Even if what we are doing is noble and productive, we can't let it get in the way of what is most important in the scope of eternity.

My friends, take heed of the lesson my grandfather learned in his life and ministry and passed along to me. Make prayer and studying the Bible a priority in your life today.

What practical steps could you take to prioritize your time with Jesus?

Dear Jesus, life throws so much at me. Help me to develop my relationship with You through prayer and study. I pray for Your blessing as I make my time with You a priority. In Jesus' name. Amen.

photo caption: Will Graham with his grandfather, Billy Graham

EARTHLY
DISTRACTIONS

"DO NOT LAY UP FOR YOURSELVES
TREASURES ON EARTH, WHERE MOTH AND
RUST DESTROY AND WHERE THIEVES BREAK
IN AND STEAL; BUT LAY UP FOR YOURSELVES
TREASURES IN HEAVEN, WHERE NEITHER
MOTH NOR RUST DESTROYS AND WHERE
THIEVES DO NOT BREAK IN AND STEAL."

— MATTHEW 6:19–20

*M*y Australian friend, Rodney, has an incredible love for the Lord and a huge heart for young people who need to know Jesus.

His testimony is one of being raised in a Christian home but straying far from Christ, getting kicked out of school, and even dealing drugs. He made a profession of faith in Jesus at a youth camp, but wasn't walking with God. A few months later he was traveling through South America when a young man on a train stood up and began boldly proclaiming the gospel message.

Through this abrupt and seemingly random—though divinely inspired—interaction, Rodney was convicted by the Holy Spirit, radically and eternally changed.

Now he lives every day to share that same hope with others.

Several years ago Rodney and I were touring the places where I

> *"Can people tell from the emphasis we attach to material things whether we have set our affection on things above, or whether we are primarily attached to this world?"*
>
> —BILLY GRAHAM

had been during my previous visits to his country. As we drove, we found ourselves on Parramatta Road in Sydney, which is lined with luxury car dealerships on either side.

To be honest with you, I'm not a guy who has a lot of vices, per se. I don't cuss, smoke, or drink, for instance. But I do love cars. Always have.

My eyes caught every color and shape as we slowly rolled past, hemmed in by the stoplights on each corner. There were Maseratis, Lamborghinis, Porsches, and more. I pointed them out to Rodney, saying, "Man, I'd love to have that car." Or, "Would you look at that one?"

As I was transfixed by the automobiles, I heard Rodney say, "Wow, I would love to be over there!"

I turned in my seat to see which car he was checking out, and I was immediately convicted.

Rodney wasn't pointing out a bright red sports car with racing stripes. He was looking at a skate park where there were teenagers in skinny jeans with hats on backward and cigarettes hanging out of their mouths, leaning on BMX bikes and cruising on skateboards.

While I was looking at cars, all his mind was focused on was ministry and the souls who are crying out for the hope that can only be found in Jesus Christ. His passion was to share Jesus with kids who are lost and wandering in a broken and dying world.

As the saying goes, we're only pilgrims on a journey passing through. That day my mind was on the temporary, the trivial, and the physical. How often that is the case with us! We want our focus to be on the eternal—as Rodney's was—and yet we get sidetracked by all the pretty things this world has to offer.

Whatever you're dealing with today, try to be like Rodney. Turn your focus away from the material things, and concentrate on what is important in the scope of eternity. Seek time with your Savior, in prayer and study, and allow Him to reorder your priorities.

What is distracting you from following
God with all of your heart?

Dear Jesus, life throws so much at me. Help me to develop my relationship with You through prayer and study. I pray for Your blessing as I make my time with You a priority. In Jesus' name. Amen.

photo caption: Will praying with Rodney Trinidad

Enduring Adversity

My brethren, count it all joy when you fall into various trials, knowing that the testing of your faith produces patience. But let patience have its perfect work, that you may be perfect and complete, lacking nothing.

—James 1:2-4

Sikkim is a small state in northeast India in the foothills of the Himalayan mountains. One of the very unique things about it—apart from being the second smallest state in India—is that it is bordered on three sides by foreign countries.

China, Bhutan, and Nepal surround Sikkim, and the only domestic way to reach it is through the Indian state of West Bengal. For those who are familiar with United States geography, I liken it to Florida. If you want to get to Florida, you must go through Georgia or Alabama. Similarly, if you want to get to Sikkim, you must go through West Bengal.

A few years back we held an evangelistic outreach in Sikkim. Unfortunately, at that same time, there was a period of major upheaval in West Bengal, which closed the roads and made Sikkim inaccessible. Air travel was not an option.

My team and I managed to make it, but there was still a problem. The band that was going to lead worship music for the event had not gotten through before the road closures, and they were stuck on the other side of West Bengal, separated from Sikkim.

Amazingly, the band was undaunted. They climbed out of their vehicle, loaded their instruments and gear onto their backs, and began walking. As near as I can figure, they must have hiked anywhere from ten to twelve miles before crossing into Sikkim.

> *"Some of the happiest Christians I have met have been lifelong sufferers. They have had every reason to sigh and complain, being denied so many privileges and pleasures that they see others enjoy, yet they have found greater cause for gratitude and joy than many who are prosperous, vigorous, and strong."*
> —BILLY GRAHAM

Such was their passion and excitement for the gospel.

I must admit that I don't always react to adversity the same way. While I know that our calling is of eternal importance, it's not always easy to jump the roadblocks—either figuratively or literally—and push ahead.

The Bible, however, tells us to not only endure hardship, but to find joy in it. Do you believe that? We aren't to get frustrated or to quit. We aren't supposed to see hardship as a closed door that means we give up.

We're to see that God is working in and through the adversity to strengthen our faith and mold us to serve Him better.

There are a few things that we are not told. We are not told that if we endure, it will get easier. We also are not told that by tackling adversity we will be guaranteed success.

In spite of all this, however, there will be joy and patience and perfection as you serve God in the midst of hardship.

We saw it in Sikkim, and I believe you will see it, too, in your own life and ministry.

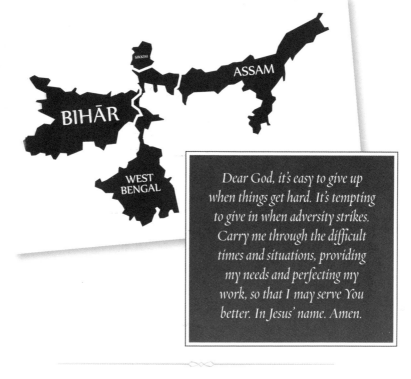

Dear God, it's easy to give up when things get hard. It's tempting to give in when adversity strikes. Carry me through the difficult times and situations, providing my needs and perfecting my work, so that I may serve You better. In Jesus' name. Amen.

What adversity have you faced in your life and ministry? Did God work in your life through it?

photo caption: Sikkim

STRIVING FOR EXCELLENCE

"LET YOUR LIGHT SO SHINE BEFORE MEN,
THAT THEY MAY SEE YOUR GOOD WORKS AND
GLORIFY YOUR FATHER IN HEAVEN."

—MATTHEW 5:16

A few years back we held an evangelistic outreach in Las Piedras, Uruguay, an historic city with a rich history.

In the years prior to our visit, Las Piedras had been in the process of building a soccer stadium. The vision for a world-class arena had been stunted, however. Midway through the project, they had run out of funds, and the venue sat incomplete.

Stretching into the sky, one could see the towering walls and the massive skeleton of the stadium, but inside the facade were merely the brackets of would-be seating, unfinished and without benches. Pillars measuring some forty feet in height stood without purpose.

Soccer matches did, in fact, take place, but everybody brought their own blankets or lawn chairs to watch. Competitions had to take place during the day because there were no lights.

Even incomplete, this would be the host arena for our evangelistic event. In an unfinished building, we would offer the opportunity for people to find their fullness—their hope, purpose, and eternity—in Jesus Christ.

> "May our gratitude find expression in our prayers and our service for others, and in our commitment to live wholly for Christ."
> —BILLY GRAHAM

As the local Christians were seeking to impact their community in a tangible manner in advance of the evangelistic outreach, they decided that the best way to do that was to help improve the stadium. Furthermore, they decided to give to their community in a manner that exhibited not half-heartedness, but excellence.

They painted the neglected concrete walls, the railings, and everything else that needed a fresh coating. The stadium sparkled with a newfound vibrancy.

Further, they collected money and purchased stadium lighting, which remained as a gift from the Christians of Las Piedras to the rest of the community, allowing the soccer teams to finally play night games.

The mayor was so impressed with what had been done to the stadium that he said the local church would always have a place at his table. It was his desire that the churches hear the needs of the city and have an opportunity to respond and be a part of the solution.

The believers of Las Piedras lived out Paul's words from his letter to the Colossians. Yes, they were seeking to make an impact, to help spread the word about the outreach and be a blessing to their city. That was their goal.

However, they didn't treat it as a task that could be done quickly and cheaply. It wasn't a half-hearted effort so they could say that they got the job done. No, they did it "heartily, as to the Lord and not to men" (Colossians 3:23). They strove for excellency. Something fitting of the Savior they served.

Of course, when their focus was on glorifying God, the whole city took notice, right up to the mayor's office.

Today strive for excellence. As you go through your tasks, projects, or meetings, in things large and small, remember that you are an ambassador of Jesus Christ. Much like the believers of Las Piedras, as you make your efforts an offering to Him, He will use you to reach others.

Dear God, help me to pursue every item on my list today as unto You, striving for excellence because I'm serving the King of kings and the Lord of lords. Give me strength, and allow me to be a light for Your kingdom. In Jesus' name. Amen.

What is one thing you can do today to take the step from ordinary to excellence?

photo caption: The Celebration in Las Piedras, Uruguay, 2010

Your One Sure Guide

Your word is a lamp to my feet
and a light to my path.

—PSALM 119:105

*M*y colleague and I had just landed in Atlanta, and we were up against the clock. We were supposed to be in Auburn, Alabama, for a meeting, but due to flight issues we had very little time to make it there.

While it's an easy, straight drive down the freeway, I decided to use the GPS that was offered in the rental car.

Now I love GPS systems, but this little machine and I were at odds from the start. We were rolling down I–20 to Auburn, but the GPS kept telling me to get off the interstate and take a different highway. I assumed the GPS wasn't updated with the latest maps, and I finally just turned it off.

Unfortunately, that was a very short sighted mistake. I'm ashamed to say that the GPS was correct the whole time, and I-20 does not lead to Auburn. Following my own path I was driving away from the destination, not toward it. The GPS was trying to redirect me to I–85, the correct route, but I was too strongheaded to heed its instructions.

By the time I finally realized my error, it was too late. We eventually made it to Auburn, but we had missed most of the meeting.

As I was contemplating my unfortunate experience with the GPS, it occurred to me that many of us—myself included—tend to treat the Bible the same way.

The Bible speaks to every aspect of our lives and gives guidance throughout. I don't believe that there is an issue in the world today that isn't addressed in some way by the Bible. The directions are there, pointing the way.

How often, though, do you stop to listen? How often do you heed the warning that it's time to turn around and go the other direction?

The fact of the matter is

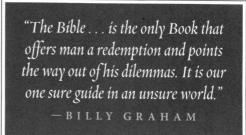

"The Bible . . . is the only Book that offers man a redemption and points the way out of his dilemmas. It is our one sure guide in an unsure world."
—BILLY GRAHAM

that Auburn was never going to be off I–20, no matter how much I wanted it to be. I could try with all my might and with every ounce of certainty in my being, and it wouldn't change the fact that I would never make it to Auburn going the route I had taken. Going my own way only led to confusion and despair.

It's much too easy to follow the path that you think is right because you feel that your way is better. Just as I was so confident in my own sense of direction, you may be too sure of your own experience and expertise to stop and see what God's Word has to say.

This leads you down the wrong path when the truth is available to you all along.

As you go about your day, seek God and His guidance. Spend time in your Bible, and be open to what God has to say to you through it. His way is always best.

What issues are you facing today, and what does the Bible have to say about which direction you should go?

Lord Jesus, forgive me for the times when I choose to go my own way, even though I know it's not the direction You have for me. Help me to seek You first above all else. In Jesus' name. Amen.

LOS ANGELES 1949

IF ANY OF YOU LACKS WISDOM, LET HIM ASK OF
GOD, WHO GIVES TO ALL LIBERALLY AND WITHOUT
REPROACH, AND IT WILL BE GIVEN TO HIM. BUT
LET HIM ASK IN FAITH, WITH NO DOUBTING, FOR
HE WHO DOUBTS IS LIKE A WAVE OF THE SEA
DRIVEN AND TOSSED BY THE WIND.

—JAMES 1:5-6

*H*ave you ever been faced with a huge decision and asked God for guidance?

In hindsight, we now know that my grandfather's 1949 crusade in Los Angeles was a watershed moment for his ministry—the outreach that made him a household name and launched decades of incredible evangelism around the world. At the time, however, the picture was anything but clear.

The crusade was scheduled to last three weeks, and God was using my grandfather to reach people with the gospel every night, but it wasn't necessarily easy. It was a struggle.

At the end of the initial three weeks, the team debated extending the campaign. That's when they received the guidance they were seeking.

A famous radio personality (and singing cowboy!) named Stuart Hamblen invited my grandfather onto his show, and even announced that he would attend the crusade. Ultimately Hamblen accepted Christ in a tear-filled moment of repentance, and my grandfather knew that they had to continue. There were other "Stuart Hamblens" out there who needed to hear the good news of Christ's love.

By the end of the fourth week, it was evident that God's hand was moving in their midst. Hamblen's salvation story was the talk of Los Angeles and inquisitive visitors began filling the sawdust-floored tent to see for themselves what was happening there. Additionally, media mogul William Randolph Hearst famously instructed his newspapers to "Puff Billy," taking the local Los Angeles story and spreading it across the country.

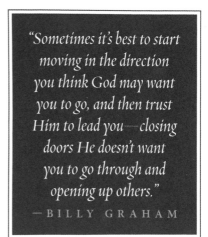

"Sometimes it's best to start moving in the direction you think God may want you to go, and then trust Him to lead you—closing doors He doesn't want you to go through and opening up others."

—BILLY GRAHAM

Soon it was standing room only, and they had to erect a second tent to fit everybody. But by the end of the fifth week they were once again facing the same question: Continue or conclude? At the same time, a massive stormfront was brewing and on track for downtown Los Angeles, threatening to wipe out the Canvas Cathedral and make the decision for them.

My grandfather and his team fervently prayed for guidance. If the campaign were to continue, God would need to divert the storm and save the tent. Much to the surprise of the meteorologists, the storm veered away!

The Los Angeles crusade ultimately lasted eight full weeks with some three thousand people placing their eternal trust in Jesus Christ. What began as a small, semi-successful-three-week outreach blossomed into something so much greater as my grandfather and his team sought God and followed His guiding hand.

What questions are you facing today?

Are you trying to make major decisions regarding your education, your ministry, or your family? Are you facing a dilemma over whether you should continue down your current path or change directions?

If so, seek God and be prepared to follow His leading.

He may speak to you through the biblical advice of a trusted friend or counselor, through a moment of encouragement or despair, through a verse of Scripture that catches your eye, or even through something completely outside of your control.

Truth be told, I'm afraid that we occasionally ask for guidance, but then ignore it because we really have our own goals and our own agendas.

As we see in James 1, however, we are encouraged to seek God's will and wisdom, but also counseled to move forward in faith when that wisdom is delivered.

My grandfather and his team did that, and many are in heaven right now because of it. I would encourage you to do the same, and trust that the Lord has a plan for you and your situation.

> Dear Jesus, I can't see
> what's ahead, but You hold
> my life in Your hands.
> Guide my steps, and help
> me to move along the path
> You have for me. In Your
> name I pray. Amen.

Are you seeking God's guidance with the questions you face today?

photo caption: The tent—nicknamed the Canvas Cathedral—that
housed the historic 1949 campaign in Los Angeles

89

MODESTO MANIFESTO

FINALLY, BRETHREN, WHATEVER
THINGS ARE TRUE, WHATEVER THINGS
ARE NOBLE, WHATEVER THINGS ARE JUST,
WHATEVER THINGS ARE PURE, WHATEVER
THINGS ARE LOVELY, WHATEVER THINGS
ARE OF GOOD REPORT, IF THERE IS ANY
VIRTUE AND IF THERE IS ANYTHING
PRAISEWORTHY—MEDITATE
ON THESE THINGS.

—PHILIPPIANS 4:8

---

*I*n 1926, a critically acclaimed book was published by celebrated author Sinclair Lewis. *Elmer Gantry* was a scathing satire of evangelists that featured a protagonist who was an ambitious manipulator with a passion for alcohol and women.

This tale was obviously on my grandfather's mind as he sat in a hotel room in Modesto, California, in 1948 and had a conversation with his team.

He recognized the negative public perception of itinerant evangelists, and he was determined that he and his team would protect their integrity as they represented the kingdom of God.

That day my grandfather issued a simple assignment to his team: take an hour to consider and catalog the major pitfalls that entrap evangelists and harm their ministry.

> "*The Modesto Manifesto . . . did not mark a radical departure for us; we had always held these principles. It did, however, settle in our hearts and minds, once and for all, the determination that integrity would be the hallmark of both our lives and our ministry.*"
>
> —BILLY GRAHAM

When the group reconvened, their lists were very similar. In short order they had a series of unofficial guidelines that have collectively come to be known as the Modesto Manifesto, which covered the issues of finances, sexual immorality, local churches, and publicity.

With integrity in their minds and hearts, they determined:

1. They would be transparent in their handling of money, forgoing emotional "love offerings" and putting the onus of fundraising on local committees.
2. They would avoid temptation—or even the appearance of impropriety—by not being alone with a woman who was not their wife.
3. They would cooperate with any local church who shared their mission to reach the lost with the gospel of Jesus Christ.
4. They would focus on integrity and accuracy in reporting numbers from their campaigns.

While the Modesto Manifesto specifically related to the role of the evangelist, I believe that we can all take something from it in our own personal and professional lives.

The initial question, however, is this: How important is integrity to you? Are you the kind of person who always tries to follow the words of Philippians 4:8, seeking that which is true, noble, and just? Do you pursue what is pure, lovely, virtuous, and of good report?

Or have you been known to cut corners, bend the truth, or venture outside the rules for your own gain?

I ask this because we have a choice. Though human instinct is to grab as much as you can, elevating yourself above others, you have the free will to decide the path you will take. The Bible makes it clear that as citizens of the kingdom of God, we're held to a higher standard.

My grandfather understood his calling, and he also realized that a lack of integrity would have eternal consequences as some would turn away rather than listen to his message. The same is true for you and me. A lost and dying world is watching. I would encourage you to live a life that is worthy of your status as a child of God.

If you were to write your own "manifesto"
on integrity, what guidelines would you include?

Dear God, help me to
live a life of integrity that
is honoring and pleasing
to You. In all things may
You—and not the things of
this world—be my focus.
In Jesus' name. Amen.

photo caption: Billy Graham and his team

How Good Do You Have to Be?

Jesus said to him, "I am the way, the truth, and the life. No one comes to the Father except through Me."

—JOHN 14:6

*W*ill," the professor said, turning his eyes my way, "how good do you have to be to get to heaven?"

I was a young student at Liberty University, a Christian school where literally everybody knew of my grandfather. Simply put, as Billy Graham's grandson, I had to get the answer to this question right.

My mind began turning. I knew that I was a sinner. I had broken God's rules. I wasn't "good." I also knew, however, that I would be in heaven one day because I had placed my faith in Jesus Christ.

I finally opened my mouth to speak. "You don't have to be good. You just have to be forgiven," I said, fairly confident in my response.

The professor quickly responded, "Will, you're absolutely . . . wrong." I didn't get it. I wasn't sure what I had missed. But then the professor made his point. "In order to get to heaven, you have to be as good as God."

In other words, if you're trying to earn your way to heaven, you can't do it. No amount of work or good deeds can make you "good enough." It simply cannot be done.

The positive thing, however, is that even though I answered the question wrong, I was on the right track with my original answer. You can't be good enough to get to heaven, but God recognized that, and it's why He made another way.

You see, some people will argue that there are multiple ways to heaven, but that's not what the Bible says. The path of "earning your way" is blocked by sin. The path that leads through other religions is absent of the Savior and His redeeming sacrifice.

Jesus showed us the narrow road that leads to eternity in John 14:6 when He proclaimed, "I am the way, the truth, and the life. No one comes to the Father except through Me."

In effect, Jesus came on a rescue mission. Knowing that God could not have sin in His holy presence, Jesus humbled Himself and became man, paid the price of our sin, conquered the grave, and created the way for a broken human being to find eternity with a perfect and blameless God.

As a follower of Christ—having surrendered your life to following the path laid out by Christ—you are not "good enough," but you are forgiven!

Now it's time to walk out the door and share that good news with others today. You're surrounded by people who are trying to earn their way or are trying to find another path, and they need to know the true hope of the simple and beautiful gospel.

Be the one who finally shows them the way!

"God doesn't say, to be perfect and you'll get to heaven. He says to confess that you're a sinner and come to the cross, and whosoever shall call upon the name of the Lord shall be saved."

—*Billy Graham*

Dear Jesus, I know that I'm not good enough; I know that I'm a sinner. But I also know that You've forgiven me, and I'm eternally grateful for Your sacrifice and victory on the cross. In Your name I pray. Amen.

If God gives you an opportunity today to share the simple hope of the gospel, what will you say?

HE MUST INCREASE

HE MUST INCREASE, BUT I MUST DECREASE.

—JOHN 3:30

*S*everal years ago on a cold, rainy morning in Charlotte, North Carolina, the groundbreaking was held for the new Billy Graham Evangelistic Association headquarters. For more than five decades the ministry had operated out of offices in Minneapolis, Minnesota, and the relocation to the town of my grandfather's birth was a sort of homecoming for him and the organization.

Part of the way through the groundbreaking ceremony, my grandfather was introduced. Slowed by age, he methodically made his way to the podium as the crowd erupted in enthusiastic applause.

For a moment he silently stared out at the crowd of admirers. Then he spoke.

His first words weren't about his successes or his love for Charlotte. They weren't about the millions worldwide who had attended his crusades. They weren't about the many great years the BGEA had in the Midwest. He didn't greet the dignitaries in the audience with proud words.

Rather, he softly uttered the words of John 3:30: "He must increase, but I must decrease." He paused, seemingly deep in thought, and then said again, "He must increase, but I must decrease."

> "Jesus must increase, and I must decrease. I sort of cringe when I hear my name called in something that I know has been the work of God through these years."
> —BILLY GRAHAM

In the middle of a ceremony meant by many to honor him, my grandfather genuinely disregarded—I would even say disdained—the attention and redirected everyone's focus to his Savior, his reason for living.

My grandfather knew that none of this mattered if not for Jesus Christ. Not one moment of the time he spent away from his family as a younger man was about him or for him; it was all to proclaim the hope of the Savior. He has even shared in the past that he wished his name wasn't the name of the organization. It makes him uncomfortable because he never wants to claim any success. It's God at work, and my grandfather always recognized that he was just a vessel.

My grandfather's attitude was a perfect lesson for all of us.

When you look at your achievements in life, in ministry, with your family or job, do you put the focus on yourselves or on Christ? Do you edge toward pridefulness, or do you seek to turn any accolades toward the One we serve, the One who gave us the ability in the first place so that we may honor Him?

I'll be honest with you: this is not easy. It tends to go against our human nature. Our innate motivation is to pump ourselves up, to cherish the spotlight, and to revel in our successes. Even while we give the glory to God, there's a voice in the back of our heads saying, *Way to go! You did this!*

What I found so interesting about my grandfather, though, is that his was a true, ingrained humility. It was a part of who he was as a servant of the Most High God.

As you go through your work today, through good and through bad, through the victories and the struggles, keep these words in mind: "He must increase, but I must decrease." You've seen what God has done with my grandfather, and He will use you, as well, as you humble yourself and lift Him up.

Dear God, pride can be a sly deceiver, worming its way into my life. Instill in me a humble spirit, that I may truly give all honor and glory to You. In Jesus' name. Amen.

Is pride a struggle in areas of your life? If so, what steps can you take to turn that over to God?

photo caption: Billy Graham and Franklin Graham at the groundbreaking of the Billy Graham Evangelistic Association headquarters in Charlotte, North Carolina

CALLED AWAY

"BUT INDEED FOR THIS PURPOSE I
HAVE RAISED YOU UP, THAT I
MAY SHOW MY POWER IN YOU, AND
THAT MY NAME MAY BE DECLARED
IN ALL THE EARTH."

—EXODUS 9:16

I will always remember the day that God called me to the Billy Graham Evangelistic Association.

In 2006, I was the pastor of a growing church plant in Raleigh, North Carolina, and in the middle of a church building campaign. Things were going smoothly. The church treated me and my family very well emotionally, spiritually, and financially. I was happy and content there.

I'd never set out to be a pastor, and honestly it was one of the last things I wanted to do. Through a series of events, however, God brought me to this point and this place, and I loved it. I had no desire to go anywhere else.

I wish I could say that I was in the middle of deep, concerted, spiritual prayer when I received a message from God, but that wasn't the case. On that fateful day I was actually mowing the lawn, and God spoke to me and said, "It's time." I felt it so strongly that it was almost like I was yanked away from the lawn mower.

Sometime later, knowing what needed to be done, I began my resignation letter. My mind was in turmoil and my heart was wrestling with this calling. As the tears flowed down my cheeks, the phone rang. At the other end of the line was an evangelist from Texas whom my father met while they were ministering to Contras in Central America. He and I hadn't visited in years.

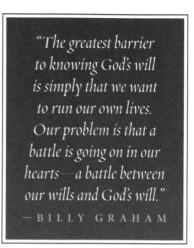

"The greatest barrier to knowing God's will is simply that we want to run our own lives. Our problem is that a battle is going on in our hearts—a battle between our wills and God's will."

—BILLY GRAHAM

"Will," he said, "God laid it on my heart to call you. I know you're in the middle of making a big decision right now, and I want to pray with you."

God further confirmed His calling to me with Scripture that He laid on my heart.

It was clear to me that it was God's will and God's timing to go help my dad at the Billy Graham Evangelistic Association.

Perhaps you have found yourself in a situation like this, when you knew that God was calling you to take a leap but you were almost too afraid or too comfortable to move.

In my case, the very clear fact that it was God's will and God's timing didn't make it any easier to leave. I loved that church, and I still love it. Telling the senior pastor of the church which had planted mine—a man who had become a mentor to me—that I was leaving was one of the hardest things I've ever done.

And the long hours and weeks away from home that I've been called to as part of my ministry with the Billy Graham Evangelistic Association have not been easy.

But when God shows you His will for your life, you must prayerfully listen and be ready to obey. Because I followed His leading into evangelism, I've had the opportunity to be on the frontline of His work around the world. I've had the incredible blessing of watching people find their eternal hope in Jesus.

God has a plan and purpose for your life too. Listen and follow, my friends. It may not be easy, but it's worth it!

Has God ever told you, "It's time"?
If so, did you follow His leading or
did something hold you back?

Dear God, I want to be in the center of Your will for my life. Help me to follow Your leading, even when it's scary. In the end, use me for Your kingdom. In Jesus' name. Amen.

photo caption: Will Graham

THIRSTY FOR THE WORD OF GOD

MY SOUL LONGS, YES, EVEN FAINTS FOR THE
COURTS OF THE LORD; MY HEART AND MY
FLESH CRY OUT FOR THE LIVING GOD.

— PSALM 84:2

The year was 1985, and the infamous Iron Curtain still hung across the doorway to eastern Europe, separating the communist countries from the rest of the continent.

Though atheism was the de facto religion of communist Romania, a crack broke open. Following years of intensive prayer and negotiations, my grandfather was ultimately allowed in to share about the God of the Bible.

From the very beginning, the tour across several major cities was an ongoing paradox, combining surprising cooperation by the communist government with regular frustrations and broken promises.

For instance, the administration of steel-fisted President Nicolae Ceausescu provided two airplanes for the team's use, as well as amplification to broadcast my grandfather's messages into the courtyards outside the churches where he would speak.

On the flip side, conflicts were abundant. Daily negotiations between my grandfather's representatives and Romanian officials would stretch into the early morning hours. The promised loudspeakers rarely materialized. At one point it was believed that the Billy Graham team would be asked to leave the country.

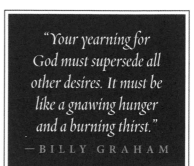

"Your yearning for God must supersede all other desires. It must be like a gnawing hunger and a burning thirst."

—BILLY GRAHAM

In the midst of the back-and-forth, however, one thing quickly became abundantly clear: the Romanian people, who for decades were deprived of the gospel, were desperately thirsty for the Word of God.

Outside the doors of the cathedrals in which my grandfather spoke, hundreds of thousands amassed into roiling seas of people who wanted to hear the good news. Many were literally climbing trees, hanging from walls and light poles, and ascending to rooftops. Such was their desire to simply catch a glimpse of the man who carried the message of the Savior. A bit like the woman in Luke 8 who just wanted to touch Jesus' cloak, the people of Romania were desperate for a small morsel of a message of Christ. The woman knew that if she could touch the living Savior, she would be healed of her physical suffering. The Romanians, likewise, knew that the only answer to the suffering they had endured was a fresh encounter with Christ.

Many of us, however, have lost that same passion, thirst, and hunger for the gospel.

That's not to say that it isn't important to us, because it is. We cling to the hope of the gospel. But you might be hard-pressed to find people willing to hang from a balcony to hear a message from the Bible.

I'm not asking you to climb to the roof of your church, but today I would encourage you to reach out your hand to the Savior. Seek Him to solve the issues that are plaguing you, and—in doing so—refresh your thirst for Him.

Are you truly passionate about Jesus Christ?
How does that passion manifest itself in your daily life?

Dear God, I confess that I
have lost some of the spiritual
fervor I once had, and I ask You
to instill in me a deep passion
for You—a thirst that cannot
be quenched apart from Your
gospel. In Jesus' name. Amen.

photo caption: Billy Graham in Romania, 1985

SITTING QUIETLY
WITH GOD

BE STILL, AND KNOW THAT I AM GOD; I
WILL BE EXALTED AMONG THE NATIONS,
I WILL BE EXALTED IN THE EARTH!

—PSALM 46:10

What was Billy Graham really like when he was away from the crusade stage and behind closed doors?" People have asked me that question quite often.

It's an easy one for me to answer because my grandfather was very much the same humble, personable, wise gentleman at home as he was when he preached to nearly 215 million people around the world.

There was only one difference. You see, though he was always speaking while in public, when he was at home my grandfather rarely talked.

This had always been the case, even in his younger days. While most visitors wanted to hear from him, he preferred to listen and learn about the person with whom he was interacting. He'd want to know about their life, their family, and their faith. He loved to hear their stories.

During the last few years of his life, as I sat with my grand-father, there was very little talk on either side. Occasionally I would give him an update and share about ministry that was taking place, especially if I had been in a city where he preached as a young man. When I would tell him about people respond-ing to the hope of Jesus, his

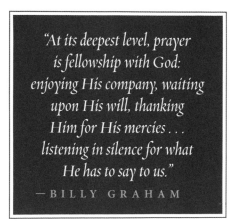

"At its deepest level, prayer is fellowship with God: enjoying His company, waiting upon His will, thanking Him for His mercies . . . listening in silence for what He has to say to us."
—BILLY GRAHAM

quiet, peaceful countenance would suddenly come alive with a deep and powerful, "Praise the Lord!"

For the most part, though, we would spend our time simply being together. That may sound odd, but it was where we were at in our relationship. And it was a beautiful thing. Words didn't need to be spoken. We could just rest in the presence of one another.

Similarly, I believe that it's vital to rest in the presence of God. Life is so hectic—schedules that are full morning until evening, jobs to do, bills to pay, phones that never stop chiming, and relationships that require ongoing development and attention.

These aren't necessarily bad things, and they are all a part of the world in which we live today. However, it can be difficult to tap the brakes and slow down when we try to spend quiet time with God. We'll race through a short passage of Scripture and our list of prayer requests, keeping one eye on the phone to make sure we don't miss that text from the boss.

I commend you for taking time to spend with the Lord, but I would encourage you to meditate on the words of Psalm 46:10: "Be still, and know that I am God."

Though the Lord surely wants you to talk to Him about what is going on in your life—your struggles and victories, your praises and your hurts—He also wants you to move beyond that and into a place where you can simply sit with Him, resting in His presence.

As you do that, you'll find the stress of the world diminishing in the hopeful peace of the One who saves, and you may discover that He uses that time to provide answers to those difficult questions in your life.

Dear God, I often feel so busy and there's so little time. Please quiet my heart and surround me with Your presence. In Jesus' name. Amen.

Have you tried sitting quietly with God? Did He reveal anything to you about the concerns of your heart as you waited on Him?

photo caption: Billy Graham

REMEMBER YOUR FIRST LOVE

"NEVERTHELESS I HAVE THIS AGAINST YOU,
THAT YOU HAVE LEFT YOUR FIRST LOVE.
REMEMBER THEREFORE FROM WHERE YOU
HAVE FALLEN; REPENT AND DO THE FIRST
WORKS, OR ELSE I WILL COME TO YOU
QUICKLY AND REMOVE YOUR LAMPSTAND
FROM ITS PLACE—UNLESS YOU REPENT."

—REVELATION 2:4-5

I remember the first time that I held my newborn daughter in my arms. I was a young man, a scared and excited new dad about to set off on a new adventure. In an instant my world changed.

It's hard to forget the "firsts" in life. They become a part of you.

My grandfather once said that the very first time he saw my grandmother walking across the campus of Wheaton College, he knew in his heart that he would marry her. I, too, remember the first time I met Kendra, my wife, while we were students at Liberty University.

On a ministry level, I remember the nervousness of preaching my first message at 2nd Avenue Baptist Church in Huntington, West Virginia. Or the first—and only—time that I shared a podium with both my grandfather and my father, which was just down the road in Charleston, West Virginia, in 1994.

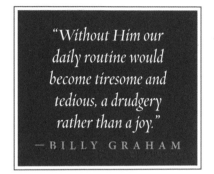

"Without Him our daily routine would become tiresome and tedious, a drudgery rather than a joy."
—BILLY GRAHAM

I remember my first time preaching evangelistically, during a small outreach in Canada, and I remember the first time walking into the Billy Graham Evangelistic Association headquarters after I had been called away from my church to begin working with the ministry full-time.

There's something that each of these "firsts" have in common, whether they're in my personal life or in my ministry. In each situation I was filled with excitement. There was a passion there that energized me. Each represented a whole new realm of challenges and possibilities. Each would help to change and define my journey.

It's interesting, though, that the excitement can wear off over time. We can still love something or somebody, but our passion begins to wane as we become comfortable.

The same can be said about our faith. In Revelation 2, we read about the church at Ephesus, which—by most accounts—was everything you would want in a church. They were faithful, hardworking, patient, and righteous. They were doing the right things.

Yet they were admonished for one thing: they had forgotten their first love. They were going through the motions, but had lost that passion that had gripped them and driven them to serve God and others.

The same could possibly be said about you. You may be floating through life with the hope of eternity, but without the passion of the Savior. You may get more excited about a mundane building project than you do about the peace that passes all understanding.

Today I ask you to remember. Remember your first love. Remember when you surrendered your life to Christ, and rekindle that relationship with Him.

When did you surrender your life to Christ?
What changed in you that day, and how can you
reawaken your hunger for Him?

*Dear God, help me today to
go back to that moment when
I first called You Savior.
Reignite the passion in me,
and use me for Your glory.
In Jesus' name. Amen.*

photo caption: Billy and Ruth Graham's wedding photo

My Weakness, His Strength

AND HE SAID TO ME, "MY GRACE IS
SUFFICIENT FOR YOU, FOR MY STRENGTH IS
MADE PERFECT IN WEAKNESS."

—2 CORINTHIANS 12:9

I stood in the pulpit of my church, shaking violently from the fever and chills.

I had just returned the day before from a mission trip to Africa. While there, I was bitten by some sort of tick, and I had contracted a wrenching illness.

To make matters worse, the previous evening—hours after I had returned from Africa—my worship leader called to say that he wasn't feeling well and that he wouldn't be there Sunday morning. In addition to being sick and facing the task of preaching, I had to hurriedly find a replacement to lead music.

Thankfully a friend of mine was available and willing. He had never guided worship like this, however. In his excitement, he lost track of time and continued for fifty-five minutes of our hour-long service!

And there I was, clutching the pulpit and trying desperately to piece together words in a way that made sense. With such limited time, I decided to postpone my prepared sermon for a week and instead struggled through a few minutes about our work in Africa. At the end—even though I hadn't preached—I offered an altar call.

Immediately a husband and wife jumped up and moved to the front of the church, saying they had decided to accept Jesus as Savior!

This story has always stuck with me, because it shows the work of God in people's hearts, in spite of our human failings.

As a minister and an evangelist, I often fall into the trap of thinking that I need to do everything—I need to prepare the best sermon, preach the most eloquently, or choose just the right passage.

While it's absolutely true that we need to give God our best, the fact of the matter is that our best isn't good enough if God isn't at work. Further, He can and will work through us even if we are at our lowest points. In fact, I believe God finds joy in "showing up" when we are out of strength, illustrating our dependence on Him.

That particular day I could barely speak. I wouldn't have blamed my entire congregation for staying away from the altar simply to avoid contact with me! But God was at work in this young couple's lives, and it didn't matter what I said or didn't say that morning. They heard God calling to them, and they ran toward His voice.

The same may very well be true in the lives of those around you. Your sibling, child, or even your coworker may hide behind a front of sin or anger, but beneath the surface God may be softening hearts and preparing them to come to Him.

At the same time, though you may feel weak or unprepared—as I was in church that Sunday—God may use you as the catalyst for their salvation. You may be the one who leads them to Christ when the time comes.

Praise God for using us, broken and weak as we are!

"We shouldn't think of ourselves and how weak we are. Instead, we should think about God and how strong He is."

—*Billy Graham*

Dear Jesus, I pray that You would be at work in the lives of those around me. In my weakness use me—I pray—as You call them unto repentance and salvation. In Your name I pray. Amen.

Has God ever used you in spite of your own weakness?

Mercy Given

For the wages of sin is death, but the gift of
God is eternal life in Christ Jesus our Lord.

—ROMANS 6:23

It was 1998, and my wife and I were on our honeymoon, driving through the unparalleled beauty of Grand Teton National Park in Jackson Hole, Wyoming.

Though I wish I had been taking my time to enjoy the splendor of God's creation, the truth is that I was cruising a bit faster than the law allows. I didn't realize it until I glanced in my rearview mirror and saw the flashing red and blue lights of a police car.

As the officer came to the window, I handed him my license and acknowledged my mistake. Thankfully, he let me go with a warning, rather than issuing a ticket as punishment for my indiscretion.

I earnestly turned to the officer and said, "Thank you for your grace."

He cocked his head and repeated the word "grace" as if contemplating the idea. "You know, that's exactly what this is," he replied. With that, he turned back to his car and drove away.

As I ponder that encounter, I view it through the lens of my faith and the gift of God to us. I've sinned. I've broken God's laws, and—in the case of my speeding—the laws of man. And yet by Christ's sacrifice and forgiveness, that sin has been taken away from me.

Many years later I do find one fault with our brief conversation that day in Grand Teton National Park. You see, I said grace, but what I really meant was mercy. Those are two similar, but different, things.

Grace is *getting* something you *did not* earn. Mercy is *not getting* what you *do* deserve.

At that moment I deserved a speeding ticket. Similarly, I deserve punishment for my sin. The first half of Romans 6:23 says, "For the wages of sin is death." That's what I do deserve, and it's a price I can't afford to pay.

Thankfully, I've placed my eternal hope in the hands of a Savior who offers mercy! I'm not getting what I deserve.

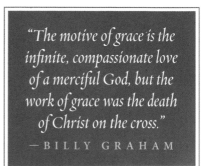

"The motive of grace is the infinite, compassionate love of a merciful God, but the work of grace was the death of Christ on the cross."
—BILLY GRAHAM

Instead I'm offered grace. I'm being given what I don't deserve. I'm receiving what's promised in the second half of Romans 6:23: "the gift of God is eternal life in Christ Jesus our Lord."

There's nothing that can be done to earn a path to heaven. I can't buy it. I can't talk my way into it. I can't get there by doing more good than bad. It is only by God's grace that He offers the gift of eternal life.

Grace and mercy are two separate things, but they go hand in hand. I'm eternally thankful that I serve a Savior who freely offers both as I call upon His name.

Dear God, I don't deserve grace or mercy, but You provide both to me as a Father giving a gift to His child. Thank You for the eternal hope I have in You. In Jesus' name. Amen.

Can you remember a time when you were given mercy by another person? Have you considered that gift through the lens of your faith and God's love for us?

photo caption: Will and Kendra Graham on their wedding day

Persevering through Criticism

"BLESSED ARE YOU WHEN THEY REVILE AND
PERSECUTE YOU, AND SAY ALL KINDS OF EVIL
AGAINST YOU FALSELY FOR MY SAKE. REJOICE
AND BE EXCEEDINGLY GLAD, FOR GREAT IS
YOUR REWARD IN HEAVEN."

— MATTHEW 5:11-12

*I*t was a leap of faith from the start. My grandfather, just five years removed from the famous 1949 Los Angeles crusade, was crossing the Atlantic on the *SS United States*. He was on his way to preach in London, then the largest city in the world.

He was discouraged and, frankly, scared. One newspaper had already written that he would "fall on his face" in London. A bishop in the Anglican church declared that "Billy Graham will return to the United States with his tail between his legs."

It was not going to be a warm welcome.

Then came the most official and strident opposition yet. Days before the ship was scheduled to dock in England, the captain received a startling news report. A member of Parliament had declared his plan to "challenge in Commons the admission of Billy Graham to England," claiming that my grandfather was using religion to meddle in British politics.

> "The Bible clearly says that faithfulness and persecution often go hand in hand."
> — BILLY GRAHAM

Still my grandfather pushed forward. Despite the saber-rattling from all corners, he was allowed to proclaim the good news in historic Harringay Arena, and the outreach is now remembered as one of the pivotal moments in his decades-long ministry.

More than two million people heard the gospel, with 38,447 making eternity-altering decisions for Jesus.

Decades later he reflected, "I put on a brave smile for the media, but I had to quietly remind myself of the spiritual truth I had learned so long ago: in my weakness, I was made strong by God's grace."

While I've never faced opposition on this level, I have encountered some over the years of my ministry. Perhaps you have as well in your Christian walk.

Especially in the age of social media and online forums, there is no shortage of loud voices mocking Christians and demanding their silence.

While it would be easy to hide from the ridicule, that's not what my grandfather did in 1954, and it's not what you should do either. Rather, press forward while clinging tightly to the promise of God's strength and grace.

As you do, remember the Sermon on the Mount, when Jesus said that you should actually "rejoice and be glad" when people revile and speak ill of you due to your faith. Why? Because great is your reward in heaven!

That's easier said than done, of course, but—if you do persevere, if you do press on in the face of adversity—you may end up like my grandfather, having the opportunity to lead others to Christ through your witness. And that's a little taste of heaven's reward, right here on earth!

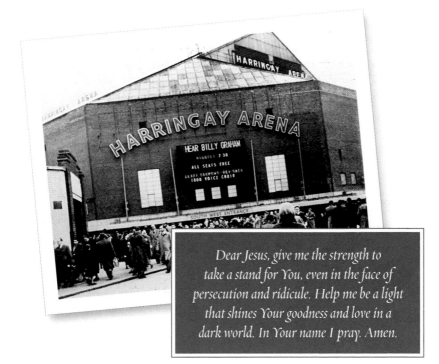

Dear Jesus, give me the strength to take a stand for You, even in the face of persecution and ridicule. Help me be a light that shines Your goodness and love in a dark world. In Your name I pray. Amen.

How have you responded in the past when people have mocked your faith?

photo caption: Harringay Arena, site of Billy Graham's historic 1954 campaign in London

SURRENDER

I HAVE BEEN CRUCIFIED WITH CHRIST;
IT IS NO LONGER I WHO LIVE, BUT CHRIST
LIVES IN ME; AND THE LIFE WHICH I NOW
LIVE IN THE FLESH I LIVE BY FAITH IN
THE SON OF GOD, WHO LOVED ME
AND GAVE HIMSELF FOR ME.

—GALATIANS 2:20

There are few things as beautiful as a glowing red campfire, flames flickering into the night sky and embers pulsing with the heat of the inferno. If you've ever gone to Bible camp and sat around one, huddling with new and old friends as you sing praise songs on a warm summer evening, you probably know exactly what I'm talking about.

As a teenager, I attended a camp in Asheville, North Carolina, not far from where I live today. As I was sitting around the fire one night, God stirred in my soul.

Though I had long since committed my eternity to Christ and had always felt a calling on my life, this was the night when I felt the Holy Spirit drawing me to give it all over to Him.

Being a Graham wasn't good enough. Going to church on Sunday wasn't going to cut it. My life, my future, needed to be placed completely in His hands. It was time to surrender.

With my eyes fixed on the fire and my heart stirred by the Savior, I stood up and moved toward the blaze. There I knelt, took a stick, and lowered it into the

> "We can hold nothing back [from God]. He must control and dominate us [wholly]. It is a surrender without any conditions attached. This surrender is a definite and conscious act on our part in obedience to the Word of God."
> —BILLY GRAHAM

flame, watching the old and dry piece of wood spring to life with a brilliant flame.

It may not sound like much, but in my mind, that burning piece of wood signified moving from my old life into one in which I was fully God's to use as He willed.

As Christians, we are called to surrender.

In fact, when I'm preaching at an evangelistic rally and I issue the invitation to begin a relationship with God, rather than using the word "commit" I often use the word "surrender." Why? Because you can commit to something, and then uncommit as soon as you get bored or it becomes difficult. Rather, when you surrender, you give everything over. Your life is now under the control of someone else.

In our Christian walk, we need to completely surrender. We need to give God our relationships, our work, our finances, and our passions; our future, our present, and our past. We need to seek His direction and pursue His plan for us with every step.

Paul paints a clear picture in Galatians 2:20 when he says, "I have been crucified with Christ; it is no longer I who live, but Christ lives in me." Now that's surrender!

Christ was crucified—He gave His life for us—and now it's our turn to surrender our lives unto Him as we die to ourselves and live for His glory.

Dear Jesus, though I love You as my Savior, I acknowledge that I don't always live a fully surrendered life. Help me to follow You with everything I have. In Your name. Amen.

Have you surrendered everything in your life? Why or why not?

photo caption: Will Graham preaching the gospel in Auburn, Alabama

LIFE ON THE ROAD

JESUS ANSWERED, "IT IS HE TO WHOM I
SHALL GIVE A PIECE OF BREAD WHEN I HAVE
DIPPED IT." AND HAVING DIPPED THE BREAD,
HE GAVE IT TO JUDAS ISCARIOT, THE SON OF
SIMON. . . . HAVING RECEIVED THE PIECE OF
BREAD, HE THEN WENT OUT IMMEDIATELY.
AND IT WAS NIGHT.

—JOHN 13:26,30

As a traveling evangelist, I get to see incredible places, meet interesting people, and enjoy unusual experiences. I've visited remote areas where shop lights were haphazardly hung on bamboo posts to light a rickety, makeshift stage. Conversely I've ventured the streets of some of the most cosmopolitan cities in the world.

It's been quite a ride, and I've been very blessed.

I also need to acknowledge that there's an emotional cost associated with this travel. I've spent countless time away from my wife and children over the course of my ministry. Caring for the souls of others has come at the expense of those I hold dearest.

Though I have a small team of people who travel with me and help in the ministry, the fact of the matter is that it can be a lonely life. Missing my family leaves a hole inside of me that cannot be filled by friends, colleagues, or meetings in faraway places.

> "I know that there is emptiness in the hearts of most people. I know that there is loneliness in the hearts of most people. They aren't sure what they are lonely for.... It's loneliness for God and they don't understand it."
> —BILLY GRAHAM

Interestingly I've noticed something else in my travels. I'm not the only person who feels this way. In fact, loneliness is one of the most prevalent human conditions, regardless of country or culture.

However, the loneliness I see most often isn't tied to the person's family. In fact, their spouse may be sitting right next to them, holding their hand. Their kids may be sitting at their feet.

No, the loneliness I'm talking about is a longing for God.

My grandfather once said that each person is created with a "God-shaped hole" in their lives, and it's a space that many try to fill with alcohol or drugs, relationships or money, work or hobbies. That empty spiritual cavern, however, can only be filled by God. Until the longing soul calls upon Him as their Savior, it remains empty.

There's a powerful passage of Scripture found in John that's easy to overlook in the context of Christ's death and resurrection, but I believe it speaks directly to this matter of loneliness and being apart from the Lord.

Jesus had just announced that Judas would betray Him, and Judas—now separated from his fellowship with God—left the gathering and walked outside.

John then says the simple phrase, "And it was night."

Those four words are both literal and figurative. Yes, it was nighttime, but that narrative also describes Judas's soul as he walked away from the Savior. Spiritually speaking, it was dark, and it was lonely.

Perhaps that describes the world for some of you who are reading this as well. You want to live in the light, but you know that you're far from God, struggling through the lonesome darkness. In your faith journey, it is night.

If that's the case, there's one remedy, and that's drawing close to God. He's right there with you, my friend, waiting for you to turn to Him.

How do you do that?

First, spend time in the Bible, which is where God will speak to you. In fact, start with the book of John, where we found today's passage, and you'll learn directly from the life and ministry of Jesus.

Second, spend time in prayer, talking to God. You don't have to be eloquent or structured. Just talk to Him as if you're talking to a friend or family member. Share what's on your heart.

Finally, if possible, surround yourself with godly friends who will lift you up and pray for you, encouraging you with the love and hope of Jesus. People aren't perfect, but in a broken world, spending time with other strong believers will help you as you grow in your faith.

Draw near to God, and He will draw near to you.

Dear God, thank You for
Your presence in my life.
When I feel alone, draw
me close to You and fill me
anew with Your presence.
In Jesus' name. Amen.

Is there anything in your life today that is
causing you to feel far from God?

photo caption: Billy Graham's car driving through the streets of Romania, 1985

Not Every Open Door Is Meant to Be Walked Through

Now it happened afterward that David's heart troubled him because he had cut Saul's robe. And he said to his men, "The Lord forbid that I should do this thing to my master, the Lord's anointed, to stretch out my hand against him, seeing he is the anointed of the Lord."

—1 SAMUEL 24:5-6

What if we knew the name Billy Graham not because of the amazing way that God used him as an evangelist? What if the name Billy Graham referred to a 1950s movie star or 1960s politician? While it seems far-fetched, either could easily have happened. Just after the campaign in Los Angeles launched my grandfather into national prominence, he found himself at a luncheon with some of the heaviest hitters in Hollywood, including Cecil B. DeMille, Anthony Quinn, and Frank Freeman, the president of Paramount Pictures.

During the conversation, Mr. Freeman asked my grandfather to consider acting in one of their films. Though I'm sure my grandfather was flattered by the offer, he quickly declined. In front of the "who's who" of tinsel town, my grandfather then shared that he had been called to preach the gospel and would never do anything else.

> *"God will never—never—lead you to do something that is contrary to His written Word, the Bible."*
> —BILLY GRAHAM

In 1964, with the temptation of acting far in the past, a different siren call beckoned. A handful of folks had encouraged my grandfather to run for president, and then word leaked to the press that he was actually considering the possibility.

My grandfather hastily ended that conversation as well. He categorically refused to run for office, declaring yet again that he was called to preach.

He was not an actor. He was not a politician. Billy Graham was an evangelist!

He had open doors to walk through, and the opportunities were likely very exciting and enticing, but he didn't go through those doors.

In 1 Samuel 24, we see David hiding out in the recesses of a cave. And who should walk into this same cave but King Saul, the very man who had David's blood on his mind. He had no idea that his prey was in the same cave and could easily turn predator.

David's men were ecstatic! This was the moment—the open

door—they were waiting for! King Saul had let his guard down, and it was David's chance to finish him off so they could live in peace and safety.

Rather than kill Saul, David merely cut a piece of his robe. Even that was too much for him, and he immediately felt troubled. He knew that Saul was God's anointed, and he had no right to harm him, even if it meant saving his own life.

You see, my friends, we often talk about God opening doors, but one needs to be very careful. Just because a door is open doesn't necessarily mean that it's a gift from God. Instead, it could be a temptation trying to steer you away from your calling and what you know is right.

If David had killed Saul, history would have been changed. If my grandfather had followed the temptation of celebrity or political power, the eternities of millions would have been affected.

My suggestion: when you see a door opening, be ready to move or ready to stay. Most importantly, though, seek God and His guidance through reading the Bible and through prayer, in order to know which action to take.

Do you sense that God is opening a door for you
to go through? If so, how is God's Word
confirming that decision?

Dear God, I want to be in the middle of Your will for my life. As doors open and close, please clearly show me when to move and when to stay, and let it all be for Your glory. In Jesus' name. Amen.

photo caption: Seoul, South Korea, Billy Graham's largest Crusade ever, with an estimated 1.1 million people in attendance on June 3, 1973

FAMILY TRAITS

*S*everal years ago a lady came up to me following a sermon and excitedly compared me to my grandfather. "You look just like Billy Graham," she proclaimed.

Jokingly I responded, "Ma'am, my grandfather is in his nineties. Hopefully I don't look like that yet!"

She quickly shot back, "No, you look like a young Billy Graham!"

"Oh," I laughed. "You mean I have a big mouth, big nose, and big ears."

She earnestly agreed. "Yeah! You do!"

Though I'll admit that I had a little fun with this sweet lady as she was comparing me to my grandfather, the fact of the matter is that it is an incredible honor whenever someone mentions the two of us in the same sentence. It's humbling when people witness some of his characteristics in me.

> "Christians should seek after holiness—without which no man shall see the Lord. Let us seek ardently the kind of life that reflects the beauty of Jesus and marks us as being what saints ought to be."
> —BILLY GRAHAM

Whether it's the North Carolina accent, the way I move my hands as I speak, or certain turns of phrase that I've picked up over the years, as the grandson of Billy Graham, I model some of his traits. It's inevitable. You likely model some of the same looks and behaviors of your parents and grandparents as well.

In the book of Lamentations, Jeremiah describes a few traits of our heavenly Father. First, God is merciful. Second, God shows compassion. Third, God is faithful.

Now, as Jeremiah is saying this, he's suffering through a time of despair. The Babylonians had just decimated the city of Jerusalem, reducing the Israelite's "inheritance" to rubble. He was surrounded by destruction.

However, those traits of God—His mercy, compassion, and faithfulness—were still so clear and strong that Jeremiah felt compelled to proclaim them.

Just as people can see a small glimpse of my grandfather in me, and perhaps yours in you, they should also be able to look at us and see that we exemplify the attributes of our heavenly Father.

In good times and bad we should be merciful, compassionate, and faithful. We would do well to exhibit holiness, love, grace, forgiveness, and righteousness.

Though they likely won't say it outright, people should be able to tell who our Father is by the way we model Him. That holds true even when faced with extremely difficult situations like the one faced by Jeremiah; perhaps even more so.

Whatever you're facing today, conduct yourself in a way that is fitting for an heir of the heavenly Father, a true child of the living God. May those around us witness the love and hope of Jesus Christ as we live our lives to follow Him.

Which characteristics of God do you feel
most closely exemplify your walk with Him?
Are there any you need to work on?

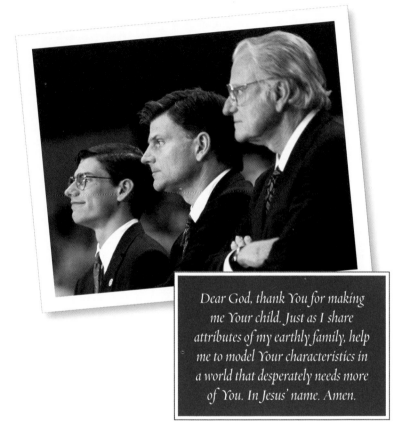

Dear God, thank You for making me Your child. Just as I share attributes of my earthly family, help me to model Your characteristics in a world that desperately needs more of You. In Jesus' name. Amen.

photo caption: Will, Franklin, and Billy Graham in Charleston, West Virginia

The Power
of Prayer

THE EFFECTIVE, FERVENT PRAYER OF A
RIGHTEOUS MAN AVAILS MUCH.

—JAMES 5:16

*O*ver the years many sought to learn the secret to my grand-father's ministry.

After all, though he was a very gifted speaker and a magnetic personality, there was very little in his upbringing to suggest that he would become well-known outside of what was then the small town of Charlotte, North Carolina.

How did this man, who milked cows by hand before heading off to school, end up being used by God to reach millions of people around the world for the kingdom of heaven?

The answer is remarkably simple.

While my grandfather was still with us, if you were to sit down, look him in the eye, and ask him the three most critical components of planning a Billy Graham crusade, he would answer, "Prayer. Prayer. And prayer."

In saying this, he would not have been joking. It wouldn't have been an attempt at being clever. It was an honest truth that is just as key to us at the Billy Graham Evangelistic Association today as it was in my grandfather's time.

> "Why do we need to pray? Because the Christian life is a journey, and we need God's strength and guidance along the way."
> —BILLY GRAHAM

In fact, when I receive an invitation to speak in a city, the very first thing I ask about is the climate of prayer. Does the community have a remnant of believers who have been faithfully praying over the course of several years? If the answer is yes, it likely means that the area is spiritually ready for an evangelistic outreach.

Prayer is eternally important, on a group (corporate) level, but also for your individual walk with God. One of the great passages of the Bible that exemplifies this is James 5.

First, prayer restores us (vv. 13–15). It brings comfort, joy, and strength. If we are broken or weak, it revitalizes our spirit. When we're downtrodden from losing battles, it lifts us up. And when we're cheerful and filled with joy, we're instructed to sing psalms and praises. All of these things restore us and fill our hearts with the hope of the Lord.

Second, prayer brings communion and forgiveness (vv. 15–16). We're directed to confess our trespasses to others and pray for each other. An example of this would be an accountability partner who walks alongside you through your victories and struggles. In doing so, we build up our brothers and sisters in Christ and seek forgiveness from the Father.

Finally, prayer brings power (vv. 16–18). James says in verse 16, "The effective, fervent prayer of a righteous man avails much." We have power when we call on the name of Jesus! You've likely seen examples of this as the "prayer warriors" in your life have been there in your hour of need. If not, look no further than verses 17–18, where James describes Elijah, "a man with a nature like ours," whose earnest prayer held back—and then brought forth—the rain.

I cannot overstate the importance of prayer to you, both in a group setting (an accountability partner, in your church, and in your community) and in your personal relationship with God. Whatever you're going through, take a lesson from my grandfather's ministry and make your first three steps prayer, prayer, and prayer.

Can you think of a time when you've found power, comfort, or joy through prayer?

Dear God, thank You for the blessing
of being able to come to You in
prayer. Help me to make my time
with You an even greater priority
in my life. In Jesus' name. Amen.

photo caption: Billy Graham and Cliff Barrows in prayer

THE SOWER

FOR AS THE BODY IS ONE AND HAS
MANY MEMBERS, BUT ALL THE MEMBERS
OF THAT ONE BODY, BEING MANY, ARE ONE
BODY, SO ALSO IS CHRIST.

—1 CORINTHIANS 12:12

Over the course of his ministry, my grandfather was given many gifts from local people in the cities that he visited. Having preached all around the world in a variety of cultures, this resulted in an eclectic collection of unique artifacts.

Perhaps my favorite piece, however, is a painting that was given to my grandfather while he was holding a campaign in Europe. At first glance, it just looks like a man in traditional peasant clothing casting seed into a field. It's so simple and understated that you might walk right by it.

However, when you stop and look more closely, other features begin to stand out.

First, the farmer in the field has the likeness of my grandfather. Second, the sower isn't alone in the field. There is another man behind a plow, breaking up the soil. Third, on the edge of the field sits a beautiful little church.

This painting is a parable, you see. My grandfather is the evangelist. He's the one who goes into the field to cast the seed of the gospel into the soil.

> *"Thinking of and serving with others can be an antidote to negative and unhealthy introspection."*
> —BILLY GRAHAM

However, as any farmer can tell you, throwing seed onto hard ground is throwing seed away. That's why the other two elements of the painting are so important. The church is there to prepare the way for the proclamation of the gospel, and the man behind the plow is breaking the ground so that the seed can land in fertile soil.

While my grandfather's name has been on banners far and wide over the past many decades, it's the people living in the communities who diligently prayed, spread the word, handled the details, and invited their friends to hear the gospel—names that we will never know—that have made it possible.

This is very much a picture of us as believers and followers of Christ as well. As Paul explains in 1 Corinthians 12, we may be different parts of the anatomy, but we are all one body.

The body isn't made up completely of ears or arms or feet. Rather, it's a complex network with many moving pieces that work together synergistically.

Similarly, some of us are evangelists. Others are teachers or preachers. We also have chaplains, prayer warriors, and those who are gifted in working with their hands.

As one body, we need each other. We're interdependent. When one part of the body is victorious, we share in the victory. And when one of us is hurting, we all feel the pain and loss.

My grandfather knew the importance of relying on the other parts of the body to break the soil and prepare the way. Regardless of which part of the body you are, strive to work with the other believers around you to reach a lost and dying generation for Jesus.

How are you working with other parts of the body
of Christ to spread the hope and love of Jesus?

*Dear God, help me to know
my role in the body of Christ.
Show me how to use the gifts and
abilities You've given me for Your
glory. In Jesus' name. Amen.*

photo caption: *The Sower*, a painting given to Billy Graham

42

GOD IS WITH YOU IN YOUR TROUBLES

THE LORD, HE IS THE ONE WHO GOES
BEFORE YOU. HE WILL BE WITH YOU, HE
WILL NOT LEAVE YOU NOR FORSAKE YOU;
DO NOT FEAR NOR BE DISMAYED.

—DEUTERONOMY 31:8

From a worldly perspective, I guess you could say I was in the right place at the wrong time.

It was December 2008, and I was about to preach in the city of Thiruvalla, Kerala.

Located in the far southwest of India, this modern, tropical city is one of the safest in the country for Christians. I was there with the blessing of the government to hold an evangelistic outreach in which I would share the love and hope of Jesus Christ.

There was one small problem, however. Our event wasn't the only "big thing" taking place in Thiruvalla. Elections were scheduled for the next day, and a group was holding a political rally in support of their candidates.

Though I've traveled extensively through the country, I'm not an expert on Indian affairs and politics by any stretch, so I didn't know much about this group. Depending upon which website you read, they could be anything from a patriotic organization that selflessly helps others to a radical faction involved in violence against religious minorities.

What I do know is that on this particular day, in this particular city, the group stood between me and the venue where I would be preaching.

Adding to the stress of the moment were recent news reports that India and Pakistan were moving toward a potential conflict, and conversations about the nuclear threat were abundant.

As I looked out my hotel room window, I saw a stream of people shouting and carrying signs, marching through the streets; a passionate throng amassed directly in front of our hotel.

Regardless of politics and talk of conflict, our evangelistic campaign was about to start, and we could wait no longer. We climbed into the car and slowly edged out onto the street.

We were immediately engulfed. Within moments our vehicle was being jostled, shaken, and bounced. Countless hands began rocking the car back and forth, quickly and violently.

I looked over at the Indian gentleman who was traveling with me, and I could see the concern and agitation in his eyes. I have to admit, that moment was the most scared I've ever been on one of my international journeys.

Here I was in the city that was supposed to be the safest, and instead I was surrounded and trapped by a mob of people. There was no way out.

You've likely faced grave fear in your life as well. The diagnosis of cancer, the dissolution of a family, the death of a loved one, or the loss of a job—all can feel as though you're trapped in a situation where you're being threatened and there's no way out.

When the struggle threatens to take hold and consume us, we need to remember the words of Deuteronomy 31:8: "And the Lord, He is the One who goes before you. He will be with you, He will not leave you nor forsake you; do not fear nor be dismayed."

You see, God was with us in that vehicle, and whatever stress or pain is gripping you today, God is with you as well! He's not going to leave your side.

As we cried out to Him in the car, the disposition of the crowd appeared to change. Instead of latching on, they seemed to move like a river around us. The flowing mass remained passionate but nonviolent as they kept on rolling.

I'm still not sure if it was the crowd that changed, or if it was our perspective and level of peace as we called upon the Lord. Either way, we were eventually able to move again, and God provided a wonderful harvest as we proclaimed His name in Thiruvalla.

Similarly, as you call on God in the midst of your troubles, He will answer you as well. The situation may remain, but He will wrap you in His loving arms and surround you with His presence in your moment of need.

"Only the Holy Spirit can give us peace in the midst of the storms of restlessness and despair."

—Billy Graham

Dear God, when I am afraid, please draw near to me. I need You. In Jesus' name. Amen.

When were you most afraid? Did you call on God in your moment of need? If so, what was His response?

43

FINDING HOPE IN THE MIDST OF DESPAIR

THEN JESUS SPOKE TO THEM AGAIN,
SAYING, "I AM THE LIGHT OF THE WORLD.
HE WHO FOLLOWS ME SHALL NOT WALK IN
DARKNESS, BUT HAVE THE LIGHT OF LIFE."

—JOHN 8:12

When I stand at the podium to preach at my evangelistic outreaches, it's often hard to see the audience. It's usually dark in the auditorium, and I have a light shining in my face.

A few years ago I was sharing the hope of Christ in the community of Orange, a town of approximately forty thousand people in New South Wales, Australia. That night there was just enough light for me to see a little child playing in the open space between the stage and the front row. I could barely make out the child's mother as she listened to the message.

After the service a small group of us went to McDonald's (which I jokingly refer to as my favorite Scottish restaurant) for a late-night dinner. As we ate, the mother from the front row came into the restaurant. She greeted us quickly and then ordered her own food and sat down.

> *"Because of what Jesus Christ did for us through His cross and resurrection, we know that we have hope for the future."*
> —BILLY GRAHAM

Following her meal she stopped by our table again. She introduced herself as Catherine and began to share from her heart.

Catherine had moved to Orange only weeks before. Her marriage was broken, seemingly beyond repair. Everything in her life had fallen apart. It had become so bad that she was contemplating suicide.

In her moment of despair, Catherine had sent out a plea for prayer via Facebook, and a new acquaintance invited her to our event.

There, she told us, she had surrendered her brokenness to Christ.

Just as Catherine had literally been sitting on the edge of darkness and light in the arena that night, she spiritually moved from the kingdom of darkness into the light of the Savior as she called upon Him.

While suicide is an extreme example, I've met many people over the years who have reminded me of this young mother. Their life is in shambles, they're without hope, and—in many cases—they believe they've gone too far down the wrong road. They feel that there's no way that God could ever love them, let alone save them.

Perhaps that's how you feel as you read this today.

My friends, God is much bigger than that! He's bigger than our sins, and He's bigger than our past. In fact, Jesus died to pay the price for those very sins that are weighing us down and causing us so much heartache.

It turned out that Catherine was related to one of the pastors in a nearby town who helped organize our event, and I have therefore been able to stay in touch with her over the years. I'm happy to report to you that she and her husband reconciled and renewed their vows, and they're living each day for Jesus.

This young mother who had once given up almost every shred of hope that she had is now a shining example of Christ's grace.

Dear God, forgive me for my sins. Fill me today with a fresh taste of Your goodness, love, mercy, and hope. Help me to rest in You and Your eternal promises. In Jesus' name. Amen.

Are you living your life with the certainty of the
hope you have in Jesus, knowing that He paid the price
and has redeemed you from your sin?

photo caption: Catherine shows Will pictures
from her wedding vow renewal service

YOUR GREATEST RESOURCE

WHAT IS YOUR LIFE? IT IS . . . A VAPOR THAT APPEARS
FOR A LITTLE TIME AND THEN VANISHES AWAY.

—JAMES 4:14

*T*ime.

It's the greatest resource that you and I have. A wealthy man cannot buy any more of it, no matter how much money he has. Scientists cannot discover or create more, and factories cannot produce more.

With every new day you have less of it than you did the day before. You can't save any today to spend tomorrow. You can't grip it so tightly that it will not slip away.

You can only use it when you have it, and then it's gone forever.

We live in a day and age of conservation, seeking to conserve electricity, the environment, even our own energy—and yet we let our time slip away, never to be seen again.

The Bible tells us a couple of key things on this important topic.

First, the Bible tells us that time is short. Think of stepping outside on a cold morning. You slowly exhale and then watch a warm mist escape your lungs, only to disappear quickly into the frigid air. That's how James describes our time on earth, calling our lives "a vapor that appears for a little time and then vanishes away."

Second, the Bible tells us how to use our short time on this earth. Ephesians 5:15–16 says, "See then that you walk circumspectly, not as fools but as wise, redeeming the time, because the days are evil." Since our time is limited, we need to be aware of how we are using it, and focused on impacting a dark world with the light of Jesus in the days we have.

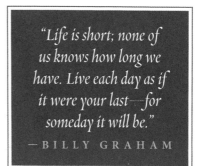

"Life is short; none of us knows how long we have. Live each day as if it were your last—for someday it will be."
—BILLY GRAHAM

Just as you are accountable for wisely using the gifts you are given, I believe you are accountable for the time you have and how you use it for the kingdom of God.

My grandfather often said that one of the greatest surprises of his life was the "brevity" of it. Here was a man who had accomplished more, visited more places, met more people, and made more of an impact than many people could ever dream of. He had used every moment well, and yet—even having lived a century—he was amazed at how quickly it slipped away.

Today is a gift, and tomorrow isn't guaranteed. For your family, for your Savior, for the sake of eternity—use your time wisely.

Dear God, I understand that time slips away quickly and there's nothing I can do to stop it. But, Lord, in the time I have left, use me for Your glory. In Jesus' name. Amen.

What are some ways that you can use your time— even recreational time—to shine a light in a dark world?

GOD'S PRESENCE IN THE MIDST OF CRISIS

DAVID WENT TO BAAL PERAZIM, AND
DAVID DEFEATED THEM THERE; AND HE
SAID, "THE LORD HAS BROKEN THROUGH
MY ENEMIES BEFORE ME, LIKE A
BREAKTHROUGH OF WATER."

—2 SAMUEL 5:20

*I*f you were alive on September 11, 2001, you likely remember exactly where you were sitting when you first received the news of the planes crashing into the World Trade Center buildings in downtown Manhattan. Countless lives were changed that day.

While it's hard to find positive outcomes from that senseless and violent tragedy, God used the events of 9/11 to inspire the development of the Billy Graham Rapid Response Team, a specially-trained network of chaplains across the country and around the world who are ready to offer hope to the hurting and peace to those in despair.

They have since prayed with tens of thousands of people following hundreds of man-made and natural disasters.

Over the years, from hurricanes to earthquakes to mass shootings and more, our chaplains have noted a sad trend. They've found that more than 70 percent of the people they seek to comfort after a widespread disaster were already dealing with some other "storm" in their lives. Cancer, addiction, the death of a family member, a lost job—crises abound and hurting people are everywhere.

> *"God is not blind. He knows about you and your problems. He knows of those who are suffering . . . and His love for His children will never leave in times of trouble."*
> — BILLY GRAHAM

In 2 Samuel, we find a crisis brewing, as well as the appropriate way to respond.

David was the freshly anointed king of Israel. He had just taken Jerusalem, a city that had proven impossible to capture over the course of many centuries. David was happy, and his people were excited. Life was good.

Now, I don't know about you, but it always seems to me that when life is going too well, something bad is likely on the horizon. It's just the nature of living in this fallen world.

And that was the case for David. As soon as the Philistines (the enemy of the Israelites) heard that David had been named king, they moved swiftly to take him out. David went from the highest of highs to the lowest of lows. His very life was suddenly at risk. This was a crisis.

How did David respond?

First, he "inquired of the Lord." That should be our initial step as well. Too often our immediate inclination may be to text a friend or to complain on Facebook. Maybe we immediately begin planning our own strategy to overcome the situation. What we need to do is pray.

Now, while there are no guarantees on when God will answer (some of you may still be waiting for God's response to a lengthy season of prayer), know that He *will* answer.

In David's case, God answered immediately, which brings us to his second step.

David obediently followed God's leading by marching into battle. He didn't send someone else or hide away in his palace. He didn't bargain or negotiate. He followed. Because of this, God led the Israelites in such a rousing victory over the Philistines that David proclaimed, "The Lord has broken through my enemies before me, like a breakthrough of water."

If life is going well for you right now, that can and will change. Now is the time to be preparing yourself spiritually for the battle that is coming.

If you're like the 70 percent of people who are already going through a crisis, know that Jesus is with you. Call on Him in prayer and follow His leading as He guides you through this valley.

As He did for David, God can bring about a breakthrough in your life.

How has God led you through a crisis or tragedy?

Dear God, when tragedy strikes
and I'm in crisis, surround me with
Your presence and show me Your
plan. In Jesus' name. Amen.

photo caption: A Billy Graham Rapid Response Team
chaplain bringing comfort in the midst of disaster

THANKFULNESS

ONE OF THEM, WHEN HE SAW THAT HE WAS
HEALED, RETURNED, AND WITH A LOUD VOICE
GLORIFIED GOD, AND FELL DOWN ON HIS FACE
AT HIS FEET, GIVING HIM THANKS.

—LUKE 17:15-16

Though many people don't realize it, months—sometimes years—of hard work go into developing a successful evangelistic outreach in a city. Several committees, manned by hundreds of volunteers, seek to cover every aspect of planning and preparation. We hold multiple preliminary events to train and energize the church. The process requires extensive relationship building and, most importantly, prayer. We do this by faith, believing that the Holy Spirit will bring a harvest as we labor in the fields.

When it is all said and done, however, one of my favorite parts of an evangelistic campaign actually comes after the evening's events are over. The musicians have left the stage, the preaching is finished, people have responded to the hope of Jesus, and I am quietly riding in a vehicle with a few of my team members, rolling away from the venue.

That may seem like an odd time to label as one of my favorites, but it's true . . . and here's why: this is when we give thanks. It's during this special time when we praise God for His faithfulness in calling many unto Himself. It's when we acknowledge that everything that has been done is worth nothing if not for the work of the Holy Spirit in the hearts of those who responded to the gospel.

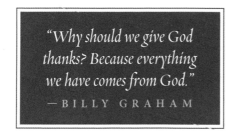

"Why should we give God thanks? Because everything we have comes from God."
—BILLY GRAHAM

In Luke 17, we see the story of ten men who were afflicted by leprosy. They were not only suffering the physical toll of the disease, but also shunned as societal outcasts. No doubt they had cried out to God for healing.

Jesus entered the city and heard their pleas, telling them to go and show themselves to the priests so they could be declared "clean." As they went—full of faith that Jesus had indeed healed them—the sores that covered their bodies began to disappear.

All but one of the men ran off, received their satisfactory checkup, and then disappeared to celebrate their new lease on life. Only one turned around and ran back to Jesus, throwing himself at Jesus' feet to thank Him for His mercy.

The lepers were physically afflicted, but you and I were once outcasts as well, spiritually lost in a dark and dying world. Similarly, when I share the gospel at an evangelistic outreach, I'm preaching to people who are in spiritual decay, praying that God will deliver them with the miracle of salvation.

Whether it's your own personal story, or a movement of the Holy Spirit as many come forward at the invitation to begin a relationship with Christ, it is a reason to fall at the feet of Jesus to worship Him.

We must never be the 90 percent who forgot to give thanks. Take a moment today to show gratitude to God for your salvation and for the spiritual healing that He has provided in the lives of others that you love.

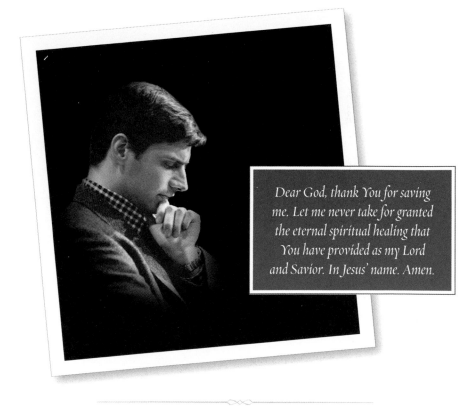

Dear God, thank You for saving me. Let me never take for granted the eternal spiritual healing that You have provided as my Lord and Savior. In Jesus' name. Amen.

When's the last time you thanked God for the gift of salvation?

photo caption: Will Graham in prayer

FREEDOM FROM THE SNARE OF SIN

IF WE SAY THAT WE HAVE NO SIN, WE DECEIVE
OURSELVES, AND THE TRUTH IS NOT IN US. IF WE
CONFESS OUR SINS, HE IS FAITHFUL AND JUST
TO FORGIVE US OUR SINS AND TO CLEANSE
US FROM ALL UNRIGHTEOUSNESS.

—1 JOHN 1:8-9

*C*an I be honest with you? I get nervous every time that I'm
preparing to step up to the podium to share the gospel.

My struggle, however, has nothing to do with the location or the
size of the audience. Whether I'm preaching to one thousand people
in Texas or forty thousand people in the Philippines, that knot in my
stomach is in the same place every time.

The issue is not stage fright. No, I've done enough public speaking
at this point that being up in front doesn't affect me, per se. The issue,
rather, is that I am keenly aware that eternity is at stake.

When I walk to the pulpit, I know that there are people in the audience who are on a path that will lead to destruction, so I pray that I won't accidentally say something that will cause confusion or deter somebody from placing their eternal hope in Jesus Christ.

I long for each person to know that sin leads to darkness, hopelessness, and hell. Even as I pray that the Holy Spirit would speak through me, I also understand that some will turn away from Christ and continue a life of sin.

And that sin has very real consequences in the scope of eternity, but also in the here and now.

First, sin separates us from God; it serves as a barrier. Think about talking to your friend face-to-face and how easily that communication takes place. Now, think about standing in two separate rooms and continuing the conversation. You may be mere inches away from each other, but you can barely communicate. That's what sin does. God is still close, but that sin builds a wall and separates us from Him.

> "Sin is the great clogger, and the blood of Christ is the great cleanser."
> —BILLY GRAHAM

Second, sin claims us as its victim. Make no mistake. Sin is tricky. It's deceitful, and it masks its danger behind a fun, enjoyable, or humorous facade. And because it has the ability to separate us from God, we are even more susceptible to falling into its snare. Once it lays claim, something that was once fun can quickly become an addiction that holds the prisoner captive.

Third, our hearts—which may have once been tender to the gospel—grow hard and cold, like calluses on our skin. Sin deadens the sensitivity so we become spiritually blind.

Finally, as we've built this barrier, fallen victim to sin, and allowed our hearts to grow cold, we become openly rebellious against God. And this is a very dangerous valley to travel.

You see, sin likes to hide behind a variety of pleasant, tempting, or humorous disguises, leading us to believe that there's something wrong with us if we don't grab hold and savor its offering. But the truth of the matter is that it is incredibly dangerous, leading us into a lifetime—and an eternity—apart from the Savior.

Today, repent of any sin in your life and return to God while there's still time. And pray for those you know who are still stuck in sin's dark trap. Hope remains in the promise of Christ!

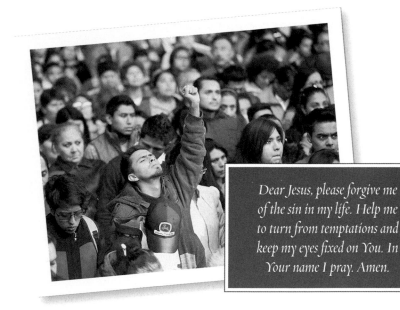

Dear Jesus, please forgive me of the sin in my life. Help me to turn from temptations and keep my eyes fixed on You. In Your name I pray. Amen.

Is sin affecting your relationship with God?
If so, what can you do about it today?

photo caption: A man worships at the Will Graham
Celebration in Pachuca, Mexico, 2017

SERVING AND SHARING

As each one has received a
gift, minister it to one another,
as good stewards of the
manifold grace of God.

—1 PETER 4:10

*S*erving others is not always easy.

Since my earliest years, my father has lead a humanitarian organization called Samaritan's Purse. One of the many great things that this group does is help with disaster response in the United States and around the world.

At any given time they have volunteers in the middle of areas that have been impacted by tornadoes, wildfires, floods, hurricanes, or earthquakes. They are putting tarps on roofs or pulling sewage-soaked carpet out of water-logged basements. They're clearing downed trees or sifting through the ashes of a fire consumed home.

It is hard, draining, backbreaking work. You wouldn't know it, however, by looking at the faces of the volunteers. As you witness their countenances of joy, you can't help but be impressed by their hearts of service.

This observation is not lost on the homeowners either. In many cases they are at their lowest points, having had everything they own in the world ripped from them in the disaster. They don't know how they're going to get through it, and then an army of strangers shows up to handle the work for them. And they're smiling too!

As you can imagine, the homeowners are often curious why these volunteers leave the comfort of their homes to serve others, and it makes an incredible impact when they share that they're helping in the name of Jesus. Time and time again homeowners have been open to having conversations about Christ simply because His followers cared enough to serve.

> *"May our gratitude find expression in our prayers and our service for others, and in our commitment to live wholly for Christ."*
> —BILLY GRAHAM

You don't need to travel to Louisiana after a hurricane to make the same impact. If you look around your neighborhood, you will see countless opportunities for exemplifying the love of Jesus.

As you do, keep a few things in mind.

First, remember to be humble. You shouldn't be serving others for your own glory. In Matthew 6, Jesus explicitly warns against boasting about your work. Rather, humbly allow yourself to be used and trust that God is working through you.

Second, be sincere and genuine. If you're trying to serve others with strings attached, you are doing it for the wrong reasons and may do more harm than good. Love and serve others unconditionally, and with a sincere heart.

Third, be consistent. While any amount of service is good, pray that God would give you the heart of a servant and provide opportunities for you to serve others. Your consistency will not only show others that your heart is truly in the right place, but it will also offer additional opportunities to share Christ's love with those who need to hear it.

Finally, as we're instructed in 1 Peter 3:15, "Always be ready to give a defense to everyone who asks you a reason for the hope that is in you." Don't be surprised if the Holy Spirit uses your heart of service to lead people to Him.

Dear God, instill in me a love for others and a desire to serve them in a way that honors and glorifies You. In Jesus' name. Amen.

What are one or two ways that you can show the love of Jesus to others by serving them?

photo caption: A Samaritan's Purse volunteer offers help and hope

169

CRY OUT TO GOD

THOSE WHO SOW IN TEARS SHALL REAP IN
JOY. HE WHO CONTINUALLY GOES FORTH
WEEPING, BEARING SEED FOR SOWING, SHALL
DOUBTLESS COME AGAIN WITH REJOICING,
BRINGING HIS SHEAVES WITH HIM.

—PSALM 126:5-6

More than one hundred years ago, my great-grandparents arrived in China as medical missionaries, spending a quarter century tending to the sick while simultaneously sharing the hope of Jesus in the area known today as Huai'an.

My great-grandparents—and my grandmother Ruth Bell Graham, who was born in China—loved the Chinese people. They sacrificed greatly to serve in the name of Jesus, even though the ministry wasn't always fruitful. There were precious few souls saved for the kingdom during their twenty-five years there.

Ultimately my great-grandmother's declining health and the ominous signs of impending conflict (what we now know as World

War II) brought their time in China to a close. My great-grandmother recovered and the war eventually ended, but they never made it back to their mission field.

A few years ago, I had the great honor of visiting Huai'an—my grandmother's childhood home—to share the gospel. Planning to preach from John 3:16, I had discovered a decades-old recording of my great-grandfather, Dr. L. Nelson Bell, reading that passage in perfect Huai'anese.

"I want someone to read this passage to you," I said through my interpreter. "I've never met this man, and many of you haven't met him either, but you might know who he is. He's going to read John 3:16."

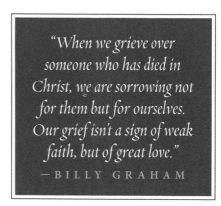

"When we grieve over someone who has died in Christ, we are sorrowing not for them but for ourselves. Our grief isn't a sign of weak faith, but of great love."
—BILLY GRAHAM

As my great-grandfather's recorded voice crackled forth in Huai'anese, with the Scripture understood by all, I heard a chorus of small gasps. The eyes of the three thousand who had crammed into the church sparkled. I could see the love that they had for my family—a love that they graciously extended to me.

In that moment I was overcome by tears.

Many responded to surrender their lives to Jesus that day, and I deeply felt that I was harvesting a field that I did not sow. It was only because of the love and sacrifice of my great-grandparents a century ago that many were now claiming the hope of the Savior.

I wish I could say that my visit to China was the only time that I've cried publicly, but that's not the case. I often weep when I see people responding to the good news of Jesus. In the scope of eternity, there is nothing of greater importance. The emotions get the best of me.

I used to apologize for my tears, knowing that they probably made others uncomfortable. Then a friend shared Psalm 126:5–6 with me: "Those who sow in tears shall reap in joy. He who continually goes forth weeping, bearing seed for sowing, shall doubtless come again with rejoicing, bringing his sheaves with him."

God used this passage to convict me. It's okay to be passionate about the gospel, and we're supposed to weep over both the lost souls who are dying without a Savior, as well as the children of God who place their faith in Him.

I'm sure that my great-grandparents spent countless hours on their knees, literally crying out to God for the souls of the Huai'anese people, and I would encourage you to do the same for those in your life who need to know Jesus as Savior. Those who sow in tears shall reap in joy!

When was the last time that you cried out to God
for something or someone? Did He answer your plea?

*Dear Jesus, thank You for hearing
me when I cry out. When we
are weak, You are strong. In
Your name I pray. Amen.*

photo caption: The church in Huai'an, China

LEAVE A LEGACY
OF FAITH

As for me, I will see Your
face in righteousness; I
shall be satisfied when I
awake in Your likeness.

—PSALM 17:15

*M*any people spend a great amount of time thinking about how they want to be remembered when their days on earth are done.

My grandmother was a spunky, quick-witted woman who loved to make jokes. One day she saw a sign on the side of the road that read, "End of Construction—Thank you for your patience."

Though I wasn't with her at that moment, I can imagine the flicker in her eye as she made the connection between that simple sign and her life. She was a pilgrim, passing through the world as an imperfect child of God. She would grow in her faith and understanding of Him, but only know perfection once she passed from this world and stood in His holy presence.

As such, the words of that roadside sign are now carved into a simple stone block above her earthly grave: "End of Construction— Thank you for your patience." She's home now in heaven with her Savior, wholly complete.

Over the years my grandfather was regularly asked what his epitaph would or should be. His desire was to be remembered as one who was faithful to God, to his family, and to his calling. He wanted to be known as a servant of the Father who walked in integrity. He wanted to be remembered as someone who was pleasing to God.

Ultimately, when he was called home to heaven in early 2018, his grave marker simply read, "Billy Graham: Preacher of the Gospel of the Lord Jesus Christ," followed by the scripture reference John 14:6.

> *"Don't let the burdens and hardships of this life distract or discourage you, but keep your eyes firmly fixed on what God has promised at the end of our journey: heaven itself."*
> —BILLY GRAHAM

Personally speaking, I'm not sure what my grave stone should say, or how I should be remembered, but I do know the promise that I'm claiming when I close my eyes for the last time on this earth. It can be found in Psalm 17:15, which reads, "As for me, I will see Your face in righteousness; *I shall be satisfied when I awake in Your likeness*" (emphasis mine).

Can you imagine that? We are so often fearful of death, but—as we look around this broken world with all of its stress and pain—we have something so much better in store for us.

For those who call upon the name of Jesus, who have surrendered to Him and made Him the Lord of our lives, we will awake to see His face one day. The suffering, persecution, pain, and sin of this world will be no more as we fall before His throne in worship.

How we're remembered in this world is important. As my grandparents have said, we want to leave a legacy of obedience, integrity, and faith, especially if it helps others find the hope of Christ while there's still time. Ultimately, however, all of that pales in comparison to spending eternity in the beautiful presence of the One we serve.

What a day that will be! And on that day I will be satisfied.

What will be said about you when your days are done?
Will your life point others to Jesus?

Dear Jesus, thank You for the promise of eternity with You. The hope that is found in You makes all the difference in this broken and hurting world. In Your name I pray. Amen.

photo caption: The stone that marks Billy Graham's burial place

About the Author

*W*illiam Franklin Graham IV (Will) is the third generation of Grahams to proclaim the gospel of Jesus Christ under the banner of the Billy Graham Evangelistic Association. Will is the grandson of Billy Graham and the oldest son of Franklin Graham.

The first of Will's crusade-style-events—called Celebrations—took place in 2006 in Leduc, Alberta, Canada. His first celebration on United States soil came later that year in Gastonia, North Carolina.

Since then he has held evangelistic outreaches on six continents around the world.

In addition to his evangelistic outreaches, Will also serves as vice president of the Billy Graham Evangelistic Association and as executive director of the Billy Graham Training Center at The Cove in Asheville, North Carolina.

Will graduated from Liberty University in 1997 with a bachelor of science degree in religion and in 2001 from Southeastern Baptist Theological Seminary with a master of divinity degree. Will and his wife, Kendra, have two daughters, Christine Jane (CJ) and Rachel Austin, and a son, William Franklin V (Quinn).